Better Homes and Gardens®

STEP·BY·STEP
SUCCESSFUL
GARDENING

© Copyright 1987 by Meredith Corporation, Des Moines, Iowa.
All Rights Reserved. Printed in the United States of America.
First Edition. Printing Number and Year: 10 9   95 94 93 92 91
Library of Congress Catalog Card Number: 86-61623
ISBN: 0-696-00735-5 (hard cover)
ISBN: 0-696-00736-3 (trade paperback)

BETTER HOMES AND GARDENS® BOOKS

Editor Gerald M. Knox
Art Director Ernest Shelton
Managing Editor David A. Kirchner
Copy and Production Editors James D. Blume, Marsha Jahns, Rosanne Weber Mattson,
Mary Helen Schiltz

Garden, Projects, and New Products Editor Douglas A. Jimerson
Associate Editors Jane Austin McKeon
Nancy P. Hall

Associate Art Directors Linda Ford Vermie, Neoma Alt West, Randall Yontz
Assistant Art Directors Lynda Haupert, Harijs Priekulis, Tom Wegner
Senior Graphic Designers Jack Murphy, Stan Sams, Darla Whipple-Frain
Graphic Designers Mike Burns, Sally Cooper, Blake Welch,
Brian D. Wignall, Kimberly Zarley

Vice President, Editorial Director Doris Eby
Executive Director, Editorial Services Duane L. Gregg

President, Book Group Fred Stines
Director of Publishing Robert B. Nelson
Vice President, Retail Marketing Jamie Martin
Vice President, Direct Marketing Arthur Heydendael

STEP-BY-STEP
SUCCESSFUL GARDENING

Editor Douglas A. Jimerson
Editorial Assistants Jane Austin McKeon, Nancy P. Hall
Copy and Production Editor Rosanne Weber Mattson
Graphic Designer Jack Murphy
Contributing Graphic Designer Mike Eagleton
Electronic Text Processors Paula Forest, Donna Russell
Contributing Writer Ann Reilly

Special thanks to Bonnie Maharam, Bill Maris,
Julie Semel, and Peter Krumhardt

On the Cover
Canterbury-bells
Photograph: Maris/Semel
Field editor: Bonnie Maharam

INTRODUCTION

Whether you're planting a hanging basket, feeding a rose, or trimming an overgrown oak tree, STEP-BY-STEP SUCCESSFUL GARDENING contains all of the down-to-earth gardening know-how you need to get the job done right. This instructive volume is designed to give you a helping hand with the nitty-gritty details of gardening. It shows you how to plan, plant, and maintain your own dream garden, one step at a time. You'll become your own expert on such subjects as lawns, ground covers, vines, shrubs, trees, annuals, perennials, bulbs, vegetables, herbs, roses, fruits, and houseplants. The book is packed with garden-tested tips and techniques that will keep your garden in top form.

Contents

GARDENING FUNDAMENTALS....6

Soil................................ 8
Water 10
Fertilizer 12
Tools 14

LAWNS.....................16

Lawns in the Landscape .. 18
Starting a Lawn 20
Care and Maintenance.... 22
Lawn Weeds 24
Lawn Pests and Diseases 26

GROUND COVERS 28

Ground Covers
    in the Landscape..........30
Gallery of
    Ground Covers 32
Dividing and Planting
    Ground Covers 34

ANNUALS...............86

Annuals in the
    Landscape 88
Sowing Seeds Indoors 92
Growing Under Lights... 94
Sowing Seeds Outdoors.. 96
Starting Annuals from
    Transplants 98
Annuals in Containers .. 100
Hanging Baskets 102
Strawberry Jars............. 104
Window Boxes 106
Care and Maintenance.. 108

PERENNIALS.......110

Perennials in the
    Landscape 112
Planning a Perennial
    Border...................... 116
Bloom Chart 118
Gallery of Perennials.... 120
Dividing and Planting
    Irises and Peonies 124
Dividing and Planting
    Daylilies and Poppies 126
Care and Maintenance.. 128
Wildflowers 130
Gallery of Wildflowers 132
Biennials in the
    Landscape 136
Gallery of Biennials...... 138

BULBS.....................140

Bulbs in the Landscape 142
Bulb Planting.............. 146
Gallery of Bulbs........... 148
Care and Maintenance.. 152
Forcing Bulbs 154
Lilies........................... 156
Summer Bulbs 158
Care and Maintenance.. 162

VEGETABLES AND HERBS.........164

Vegetables in the
    Landscape 166
Vegetable Garden
    Planning 170
Vegetable Techniques .. 172
Small-Space Gardens 174
Raised-Bed Gardens..... 176
Getting Started 178
Extending the Season ... 180
Care and Maintenance.. 182
Insects and Diseases 184
Herbs 186
Gallery of Herbs.......... 188
Care and Maintenance.. 190

VINES 36

Vines in the Landscape ... 38
Gallery of Annual and
    Perennial Vines 40
Care and Maintenance 42

SHRUBS 44

Shrubs in the Landscape   46
Gallery of Shrubs 50
How To Plant a Shrub ... 58
Pruning Shrubs 60
Hedges 62
Care and Maintenance.... 64

TREES 66

Trees in the Landscape ... 68
Gallery of Trees 72
How To Plant a Tree 78
Pruning Young Trees 80
Pruning Older Trees 82
Care and Maintenance.... 84

ROSES 192

Roses in the Landscape 194
Rose Classification 196
How To Plant a Rose ... 200
Pruning Roses 202
Care and Maintenance .. 204
Insects and Diseases 206

FRUITS AND BERRIES 208

Fruit in the Landscape .. 210
Selecting Fruit Trees 212
Planting and Pruning
    Fruit Trees 214
Espalier Pruning 216
Care and Maintenance .. 218
Cane and Bush Fruits ... 220
Care and Maintenance .. 222
Grapes 224
Strawberries 226
Care and Maintenance .. 228

INDOOR GARDENING 230

Gardening Indoors 232
Gallery of Houseplants 234
Gardening Under
    Lights 238
Plant Propagation 240
Care and Maintenance .. 242
Insects and Diseases 246

CONSIDER YOUR CLIMATE 248

CREDITS 250

INDEX 252

GARDENING FUNDAMENTALS

Gardening, some say, is a declaration of hope in tomorrow. It's true that without hope, no one would work the soil, or plant the seeds, or wait for seeds and plants to burst into flower or fruit. Yet hope alone won't guarantee success in the garden. A gardener's success requires a sound knowledge of the basics of plant life—how plants grow, and what light, water, food, and soil they need. When you nurture plants, with loving hands guided by your knowledge of gardening fundamentals, you can turn today's hope into tomorrow's beauty. Good luck!

SOIL

Every gardener wishes for large and healthy plants, big, bright flowers, luscious, record-breaking vegetables, and juicy, mouth-watering fruits. Such blue-ribbon gardening results require some commonsense techniques; more important, they depend on one basic ingredient: good soil. By starting from the ground up, you can help provide the essentials to give plant roots space, water, food, oxygen, and minerals for ideal growing conditions.

TYPES OF SOIL
■ In order to know how to treat your soil properly so it will do its best for you, you need to know a little about its texture. Soil consists of three types of particles: sand, the largest; clay, the smallest; and silt, which falls in between. The ideal soil—loam—balances all three types.

Sandy soils dry out quickly and leach fertilizer rapidly, but these soils drain well. Clay soils are heavy, hold excessive water, and have poor aeration, yet hold on to fertilizer well. Soil that is heavy with clay will stick to your shovel; when the soil is moist, you can squeeze it with your fingers into a tight ball.

SOIL IMPROVEMENTS
■ You'll rarely find ideal soil in your garden, but you can improve what you find to achieve healthier plant growth and better produce. The secret to soil improvement lies in organic matter, in the form of peat moss, leaf mold, manure, or compost. You should work in enough organic matter to make it about 25 percent of your finished soil.

If possible, add organic matter in the fall to give the microorganisms in the soil plenty of time to decompose the material before spring planting. After working in organic matter, add any other amendments, such as bonemeal or superphosphate for good root growth. Spade or till soil to a depth of 12 to 24 inches, breaking large chunks into smaller particles. You can also improve soil with double digging, which switches richer topsoil to the root zone.

UNDERSTANDING pH
■ The term pH measures how the soil fits on the acidic-basic scale, indicated by a number between 0 and 14. The

number 7 is neutral, with 0 being most acidic and 14 most basic. The pH is important because nutrient availability, soil organisms, and solubility of toxins depend on it. Although some plants like a low pH, most prefer a pH between 6 and 7. A pH that is too low should be raised with ground dolomitic limestone; one that is too high can be lowered with sulfur. Gypsum will condition soil without affecting pH.

Because you can't tell what's in soil by looking at it, it's a good idea to have your soil tested every few years. A simple test will indicate pH. Other tests can be run for organic matter and nutrients. Collect the soil from several areas, being careful not to include mulch, thatch, or roots. Mix the soils together in a quart jar. Labs, county agents, and some garden centers test soil, or you can do it yourself with a purchased kit.

Water

Mother Nature provides us with water in the form of rain, dew, and underground sources. Sometimes, however, these natural sources aren't enough. Extreme heat and wind, for example, make soil moisture evaporate very quickly. When temperatures soar or winds increase, plants will lose greater amounts of water through their leaves, and you'll need to replenish the water more often.

HOW MUCH, HOW OFTEN
■ Gardeners often ask the question, "How often should I water, and how much should I apply?" There isn't a simple answer. Soil texture is a key factor; clay soils can hold three times as much water as sandy soils, and will not need to be watered as frequently. Improving your soil as described on pages 8 and 9 will allow the soil to use and conserve water most efficiently.

As a rule of thumb, apply one inch of water per watering, and don't water again until the soil surface dries. The time it takes to apply one inch of water depends on your method of watering and your water pressure. A simple and inexpensive way to find your watering time is to set out a rain gauge or several empty cans, and time how long it takes to collect an inch of water, using your watering method.

WATERING TECHNIQUES
■ For best results, water to soak the soil deeply. Light and frequent waterings use more water and encourage shallow roots, making your plants more vulnerable to damage from drought, weeds, and diseases. Deep waterings lead to desirable long roots.

To prevent sacrificing moisture to evaporation, avoid watering on a windy day. If your garden is in an exposed location, install a hedge or windbreak to temper the wind's force. Remember also that because large trees rob water from smaller shrubs nearby, you may need to apply extra water. Street-side trees, surrounded by pavement, often do not receive enough water. You can help by digging a well, which will collect water, around the trunk.

WATERING METHODS
■ The system you choose to water your garden depends on your property, preference, and budget. If you use oscillat-ing or rotating sprinklers, be sure that the watered areas overlap. Water during cool morning hours, when less moisture will dissipate. Early watering also lets foliage dry before evening, which prevents fungus diseases.

A sprinkler needs a garden hose to get the job done. Hoses come in a variety of sizes: the ½-inch hose is lightweight; the ⅝-inch hose is the most common size; and the ¾-inch hose is for heavy-duty work. To prevent kinks, store all hoses rolled up. Empty hoses in the fall before storing for the winter.

Watering by hand is time-consuming and inefficient for large areas, but necessary for container plants, new seedlings, and hanging baskets.

A newer system, referred to as drip irrigation, has recently become popular. In this system, water travels to the plants through tiny holes in a hose laid on the ground, or by small extenders from the main hose. Drip irrigation takes longer, but uses 30 percent less water and produces better growth.

MULCHING
■ To conserve moisture in the soil and cut down on the amount of supplementary water needed, lay a 2- to 3-inch

layer of mulch on the ground surrounding plants. A mulch will also keep down weeds (which compete for soil moisture), and looks attractive. Recommended mulches include shredded bark, grass clippings, straw, pine needles, leaf mold, bean hulls, or a layer of black plastic. Organic mulches have the added benefit of enriching the soil as they decompose.

FERTILIZER

Plants are like the people that care for them. They are born, they grow, they reproduce, and they die. During this process they need light, water, food, air, and the right temperature to survive and thrive. We can't always control all of the elements in our plants' environment, but we can be certain that they receive the right nutrition. Knowing their fertilizer needs is important.

THE ELEMENTS

■ Good plant growth requires 16 basic elements. If any of these elements are missing or not present in the correct amounts, plants will grow poorly, and produce fewer and smaller flowers and fruits. The necessary elements include carbon, hydrogen, nitrogen, phosphorus, potassium, calcium, magnesium, sulfur, and minor elements such as manganese, copper, zinc, molybdenum, chlorine, boron, and iron.

Water and air provide plants with carbon, hydrogen, and nitrogen. Many other elements also naturally abound and are not a matter for concern. Nitrogen, phosphorus, and potassium form a "complete" fertilizer and need to be regularly added to soil.

Nitrogen (N) is found in every plant cell as a part of many proteins and of chlorophyll. It encourages vegetative growth and contributes to a dark green color. Phosphorus (P) stimulates root growth and is vital to photosynthesis. It plays a key role in flowering and fruiting. Potassium (K) has a role in metabolism, contributes to hardiness and disease resistance, and affects respiration and transpiration.

Calcium is needed for new growth. If it isn't adequately present in your soil, you can apply it through lime or gypsum. Dolomitic limestone, the best, also contains magnesium, needed for enzyme action and for moving phosphorus through the plant. Sulfur, an important component of plant protein, is available from air, water, organic matter, or application. Trace (or minor) elements, so named because they are needed in small doses, play a role in photosynthesis, enzyme action, overall plant growth, and nutrient absorption. All complete fertilizers contain N, P, and K and often other elements.

ORGANIC VS. INORGANIC

■ Fertilizers are classed as organic or inorganic. True organic fertilizers come from animal and plant wastes. Examples are blood meal, manures, and cottonseed meal. Organic fertilizers are slow-acting and nonburning, but are bulky, often low in nitrogen, and unpredictable in their nutrient release.

Inorganic fertilizers are chemicals such as potassium, ammonium nitrates, and ammonium phosphates. They are very water soluble, but can burn and leach quickly. If you apply inorganic fertilizers in concentrated amounts, keep them from direct contact with roots and foliage to avoid killing the plants instead of nurturing them.

A group of fertilizers called synthetic organics—such as urea, ureaformaldehyde, and IBDU—release nutrients slowly, based on water or soil temperature. They burn and leach less.

On fertilizer labels, you'll see numbers such as 10-6-4, 5-10-5, or 20-20-20, which stand for the percentages of N, P, and K in that order. Use a high N for lawns, a high P for flowering or fruiting plants, or a balance for foliage. You'll also see the term WIN, which stands for Water Insoluble Nitrogen. A WIN of less than 15 percent means a fast-acting fertilizer, and one over 30 percent releases slowly.

HOW TO APPLY

■ Apply granular fertilizers to soil by hand or with a spreader, and work them into the top two or three inches of soil, being careful not to damage shallow roots. Apply fertilizers evenly over the root area; avoid applying fertilizer to the stem or crown of plants. Liquid fertilizers should be applied to the soil or foliage. To avoid burning plants, water well beforehand and do not apply too much fertilizer.

Large trees and shrubs can be fed by driving plant spikes into the ground or by injecting fertilizer with a root feeder. Because the majority of a tree's feeder roots—the ones that can use nutrients—lie in the top 10 to 12 inches of soil, feeding too deeply will not help get the nutrients to the right place.

WHEN TO APPLY

■ Fertilize plants when growth is at its peak or when they're producing flowers or fruits. Don't encourage late summer growth, because it can be harmed by oncoming cold weather. One popular method is late-fall dormant feeding. With this method, fertilizer is applied after plants stop growing, and remains in the soil over winter so it can be used when root growth starts in early spring.

TOOLS

Choose the right tool for the job. That sage advice is as true in the garden as it is in the workshop indoors. A high quality tool will last longer; it also will make gardening easier and more enjoyable. Most tools come in a variety of styles and sizes. They may have short or long handles, and round or square surfaces. At the store, try the tools out for grip and reach before you buy.

SPADES AND SHOVELS
■ A spade is a kind of shovel. There are many types of spades to choose from. Use rounded, pointed, or straight, flat blades for digging and mixing soil, or working in organic matter and fertilizer. A shovel has a rounder blade and works best for lifting and moving soil or other materials.

When using a spade, push it down into the soil with your foot, push back on the handle, and roll soil to the side. Keep the blade clean, free of rust, and oiled. Tap out nicks with a hammer.

TROWELS
■ Trowels are hand tools for planting annuals, perennials, bulbs, and other small plants. Long, narrow trowels work best for digging holes in tight places. Invest in a good trowel, because the shaft can bend easily on inexpensive types. As with shovels, keep trowels clean and oiled.

HOES
■ Hoes break up soil and remove weeds, a technique called cultivation. Hoes can be flat across or have curved fingers. To use a hoe, pull the cutting edge toward you, taking up weeds at the same time. Keep your hoe sharp by using a file or a grinding wheel. Dull hoes bend weeds but don't cut them.

RAKES
■ Rakes have a multitude of uses, from smoothing soil and seedbeds to removing leaves and other debris from lawns. Leaf and grass rakes are usually made of bamboo or metal. Large rakes will help you get leaves cleaned up quickly in the fall; small rakes (or rakes that are adjustable) will help you get into those hard-to-reach spots under bushes or in window wells.

SPADING FORKS
■ When digging perennials, tubers, or bulbs for dividing, use a spading fork. It helps loosen the soil around the roots without damaging them. Because the tines will break up clumps easier than a spade will, this tool also comes in handy for digging through very heavy garden soil.

TOOLS FOR PRUNING
■ Standard pruning shears can be either the blade-and-anvil type or hook-and-blade type, and are used for cutting trees, shrubs, or stems up to about the thickness of a pencil. Make larger cuts with loppers, which have long handles for added leverage. Look for pruning saws and pole pruners to use on thick

and hard-to-reach branches. For very large branches or big pruning jobs, consider either a hand or power chain saw to make the task easier.

For shaping hedges, choose one of the many hedge clippers available. If you're short—or your hedges are tall—try clippers with extra-long handles. For trimming areas where the lawn mower won't reach, use special grass shears or string weeders and trimmers; don't use them for tougher jobs because they may break easily.

LAWN MOWERS

■ Walk-behind mowers are best suited for lawn care on small lots or on yards with a profusion of trees, fences, or other solid obstacles. Consider an electric mower if your yard is less than 10,000 square feet. (Cord length will reach this area.) For large, unobstructed lawns, you'll save time and energy if you make an extra investment in a riding mower or a self-propelled, walk-behind type.

15

LAWNS

The grass can be much greener on *your* side of the fence if you properly care for it. A well-maintained lawn will help frame your home with a lush carpet of green all summer long. To grow a healthy, good-looking turf without investing a lot of time and effort, take advantage of modern chemistry and horsepower. New seed formulations, fertilizers, and pest killers are now available to help you start a new lawn or improve an old one quickly and easily. And new, improved power mowers, trimmers, spreaders, rakes, and other lawn tools make fast work of regular turf maintenance.

LAWNS IN THE LANDSCAPE

A beautiful lawn begins with careful planning. The type of grass you plant will depend largely upon your landscape design and how you plan to use the lawned area. Formal flower borders should be set off by a complementary, fine-textured turf that is kept edged and closely manicured. A durable, coarser turf is more appropriate for an area that gets a lot of traffic or is used by children for play. An informal setting doesn't require meticulous upkeep.

SEED VS. SOD

■ Starting from seed is the most economical way to grow a lawn, but this method requires attention to planning, preparing, planting, and watering. If you have an area where seeding is difficult, such as a slope, or you want a lawn in a hurry (and are willing to spend more money), sodding is the route to follow. Some of the warm-season grasses should be started with stems or sod.

CHOOSING THE RIGHT MIX

■ Your climate is a big factor in what grasses you choose. Grasses are generally described as cool-season for the northern part of the country, and warm-season for southern areas. Cool-season grasses grow best in spring and fall; warm-season types grow fastest in summer and are not as winter-hardy.

Mixtures of several grass types work best for most lawns. That way, even if disease strikes, the damage probably will be limited to just one of the grasses in the mixture. By mixing a spring performer with a drought-tolerant summer grower, you'll help your lawn look good all year. To be sure of success when seeding a new lawn, choose a high-quality seed mixture containing very little "crop" or weed seeds. Bargain brands may germinate poorly.

COOL-SEASON GRASSES

■ Among the best cool-season types are: *Kentucky bluegrass*—One of the most popular. It requires moderate care to grow dense, dark, and medium-textured. *Fescue*—Usually combined with bluegrasses, it tolerates shade and dry conditions, and seldom needs fertilizing. *Tall fescue*—Relatively new in popularity, this grass is drought-tolerant and excellent for high-traffic areas. *Perennial ryegrass*—Quick growing and tough. It makes a fine-textured lawn when mixed with Kentucky bluegrass. *Bent grass*—Needs frequent watering and fertilizing. Best used for a golf course.

WARM-SEASON GRASSES

■ Recommended warm-season grasses are: *Bermuda grass*—Most drought-tolerant. Its excellent wearability makes it a good choice for play areas. *St. Augustine*—Good for shade. This is a coarse, nondurable grass. *Zoysia*—Heat- and drought-resistant, but late to turn green in the spring. Sometimes used in northern lawns for its toughness.

MOWING TECHNIQUES

■ You'll need to mow your lawn regularly to keep it looking its best. Cutting height depends on the type of grass and the time of year. Mow often enough so that not more than one-third is cut off at one time. In shady spots, cut grass less frequently and at a height of ½ inch taller than normal. Keep the blades of your lawn mower sharpened to avoid damaging grass tips.

STARTING A LAWN

The best time to start a new lawn is in the spring or early fall, when days are cool and moist and weeds are less of a threat. Seeding in early fall often provides the best results because it gives the lawn time to become well established before heavy frosts hit.

The first step in starting a lawn from scratch is to properly prepare the soil. (See opposite page.) To be sure of your soil conditions, have your soil tested for fertility and pH. Adequate levels of phosphorus and potassium are important for vigorous root growth, so you'll want to add these nutrients if the soil test shows they're needed. The ideal pH for lawns is between 6.0 and 7.0. If you need to raise the pH, use dolomitic limestone at the rate of 50 pounds per 1,000 square feet. If you need to lower it, use powdered sulfur.

Broadcast seeds with a mechanical spreader at the rate recommended on the seed package; overseeding will cause the tiny grass plants to choke each other out. Mix the seeds in the hopper before spreading. Apply one-half of the total amount of required seed in one direction and the second half at right angles to the first. Rake the area lightly to barely cover the seeds with soil.

If you have access to a roller, roll the seedbed to guarantee that all seed comes in contact with the soil. Water gently but deeply. Continue to water every day (or whenever the soil looks dry) until 3 weeks after the seeds germinate. To prevent seeds from washing away, water slowly to keep the soil evenly moist. When the grass is 2 to 2½ inches tall, mow it to a height of 1½ to 2 inches; mow regularly thereafter.

1 If the existing soil is poor, add 4 to 6 inches of topsoil or sphagnum peat moss. Cultivate with a rotary tiller or spade to a depth of 4 inches.

2 After removing any stones, twigs, or other debris, rake the surface as level as possible. If liming is necessary, incorporate the lime into the soil prior to leveling.

Sod (*above*) will give you an instant lawn. Unlike seeds, sod will establish itself fast and with little competition from weeds. Bluegrass sod is the best because it quickly weaves a close-knit, vigorous, and attractive turf.

When you choose sod, look for well-rooted, moist rolls that are uniformly green and not yellowing. After you get the sod home, install it as soon as possible, especially during very hot weather; don't let more than 2 to 3 days go by, even in cool weather. Store the sod in a cool, shaded area and moisten it if it starts to dry out before being laid.

Prepare the soil as you would for seeding. The soil under the sod should be moistened before it's laid, and the lawn should be kept watered for several weeks until the grass is established. Sodding can be done even in the summer, provided you keep the sod moist.

3 Apply lawn fertilizer at the rate of 2 pounds of nitrogen per 1,000 square feet. For even distribution, use a clean drop spreader.

4 After these tasks are completed, water the area thoroughly with a gentle spray from a garden hose to allow the soil to settle.

Some grasses, such as zoysia, bermuda grass, and St. Augustine, are sold as plugs (small sections of sod) or sprigs (pieces of stem taken from sod). Plant these in early spring, up to 12 inches apart; keep moist before planting.

CARE AND MAINTENANCE

Your lawn will need a little extra help if you want it to wear well and look its best. Follow these tips for a healthy turf.

WATERING

■ Water requirements for lawns vary depending on soil, rainfall, and type of grass. A lawn with sandy soil will need to be watered more often than one with clay soil. Some cool-climate grasses, like bluegrass, will need more water than drought-tolerant types, such as fescue.

Your lawn will show these signs when it's dry and needs water: (1) grass turns from a rich green to a bluish cast; (2) turf loses resiliency so footprints remain longer; and (3) growth is substantially slowed. To encourage deep roots, water to a depth of at least 6 inches.

FERTILIZING

■ A fertilizer rich in nitrogen, phosphorus, and potassium will help keep your lawn looking lush. In the spring, apply a fertilizer with a nutrient ratio of 2-1-1. For most lawns, 1 pound of nitrogen per 1,000 square feet is plenty. Feed again in the fall, in the ratio of 1-2-2, to encourage healthy root growth before the ground freezes. Nitrogen applied before winter should be the water-insoluble, slow-release kind.

THATCH REMOVAL

■ A small amount of thatch—an accumulation of dead stems and roots—is beneficial to a lawn because it becomes an organic fertilizer as it breaks down. A heavy buildup of thatch, however, prevents penetration of moisture and nutrients into the soil and may harbor insects and disease. To keep thatch at a healthy level, remove excess material once a year with a power rake.

Don't let leaves or other objects (such as lawn furniture and toys) remain on the lawn for any longer than necessary, or the grass under them will quickly lose color.

For even distribution, apply fertilizer with a spreader instead of by hand. To avoid lines, apply half of the fertilizer in one direction and the other half at right angles.

If you're cutting an area out of the lawn for a new flower bed or patio, you may want to save the sod and relocate it to a sparse area. To lift the sod, place a flat spade under the roots, cut, and roll.

Repairing bare spots is like starting a new lawn. Remove dead grass, improve the soil, fertilize, lime if needed, seed or sod, and water regularly. Avoid walking on the new grass until it's established.

LAWN WEEDS

Name	Comments	Controls
Chickweed, Mouse-Ear *Cerastium*	Creeping perennial that forms dense matlike growth. Tiny white flowers appear from April into October. Prefers moist, cool conditions. Grows in most areas except along Mexican border or in North Dakota.	Difficult to pull, because it entangles in the grass. Control by applying a postemergent herbicide.
Crabgrass, Common *Digitaria sanguinalis*	An annual grass found across the country, except in the Southwest and southern Florida. Blooms July to October. Doesn't grow in shade—likes moisture and sun. Seeds mature in late summer and early fall.	Follow a good cultural schedule to choke out. Mow lawn high during spring to shade germinating seedlings. Apply a preemergent control in early spring.
Dandelion *Taraxacum officinale*	Found across the country except in a few areas of deep South. Produces coarse-toothed, long leaves in bunch and yellow blooms, followed by round white seed heads. In cold areas, flowers from March until frost.	The entire taproot must be dug out; otherwise, a new plant will grow. Use a postemergent herbicide in fall. Spot chemical applicators are available for use in spring and summer.
Dock, Curly *Rumex crispus*	A perennial with a 1½- to 2-foot taproot. Produces one or more tall stems. Found across the country. Its spikes of whitish flowers appear from June into September.	If infestation is small, dig it out, being sure to get the entire taproot. On larger area, apply a postemergent herbicide. Apply spray into each plant crown for best results.
Lamb's-Quarters *Chenopodium album*	Common annual weed. Leaves are gray-green on top and have white underside. Occurs most in newly seeded lawns or lawns with thin turf. Plumelike whitish flower heads and seeds appear from June to October.	Mow lawn closely. Soak soil for easy pulling. For large area, use postemergent herbicide.

Name	Comments	Controls
Plantain, Broad-Leaved *Plantago major*	A perennial (sometimes annual) with broad leaves, 3 to 6 inches long and bunched low to ground. Tall, slender stalks bear pencil-shaped flowers from June to October. Found across the country. Spreads by seeds.	If infestation is small, dig it out when soil is moist. For a larger area, use a postemergent herbicide in the early spring or fall.
Quack Grass, or Couch Grass *Agropyron repens*	A hardy, vigorously spreading perennial bunchgrass. Forms a dense root structure by rooting at every joint on underground stems. Found across the country except in parts of the Southwest and deep South.	Cannot be eradicated without killing lawn grasses, too. A black plastic cover extended over a patch will starve all growth. Or apply a postemergent control; wait three weeks before reseeding lawn.
Shepherd's Purse *Capsella bursa-pastoris*	A persistent annual that forms a circle of low leaves with white flowers on tall stems. Seedpods are flat and heart-shaped like a shepherd's purse.	Fairly easy to pull if soil is moist. Soak soil before pulling. For larger area, use a postemergent herbicide.
Thistle, Canada *Cirsium arvense*	Thrives in clay soils in the North. Long prickly leaves and lavender flowers. Spreads by seeds and underground roots. Blooms July through October.	Use knife to cut belowground and remove crown from roots. For larger infestation of this weed, apply a postemergent herbicide.
Yarrow, Common, or Milfoil *Achillea millefolium*	Creeping perennial with very finely divided, soft leaves and white cushiony blooms. Grows in most regions with poor soil, except in the Southwest. Spreads by seeds and underground stems.	Dig weed out as soon as it appears. For larger area, control by a couple of applications of postemergent herbicide during the growing season.

LAWN PESTS

Insect	Description and Trouble Signs	Controls
Armyworms	These pests are found in dense groupings, feeding on grass to make a somewhat circular area. The caterpillar is up to 1½ inches long with green, tan, or black stripes on its back. Causes damage from spring through late summer.	Keep lawn healthy by watering and feeding on a regular schedule. Apply a slow-release urea-formaldehyde lawn fertilizer. Control pest with Diazinon at first sign of extensive feeding.
Billbugs	Adults are ¼ to ¾ inch long, black or reddish-brown beetles with long snout. They chew holes in stems of grass, depositing eggs in them. Eggs hatch into chunky, legless, ½-inch-long larvae, which puncture stem and crown as they feed. They kill grass in patches; grass blades break off at soil line.	In lawns with a history of billbug damage, treat in the early spring with Diazinon or carbaryl to control adult beetles. Or, treat in the early summer to control larvae.
Chinch bugs	Adults have black bodies with white wings and reddish legs. Nymphs grow from very small size to ⅛-inch-long adults. They prefer dry, sunny areas. Chinch bugs feed at all stages of their development, leaving large yellowish-to-brown patches.	Well-fed lawns discourage this pest. Treat the two generations of this insect in June and August with Diazinon or carbaryl.
Cutworms	Smooth grayish or brownish caterpillars, up to 2 inches long; feed at night after hiding under protective covering during the day. They cut off grass at the soil line and can be a problem from spring until late summer. Cutworms eat away grass stems at soil surface, leaving small dead spots.	If affected area is small, it can be puddled with water to bring worms to the surface to collect and destroy. Control with carbaryl or Diazinon.
Grubs, White	Grubs are the larvae of beetles, including Japanese and June beetles. Larvae are thick, whitish, C-shape underground worms that vary from ¾ to 1½ inches in length. Grubs eat grass roots, leaving brown, dead patches easily lifted out of the lawn.	In small areas, cut away sections of sod; pick and destroy grubs from underside. In severe infestations, control with Diazinon.

Insect	Description and Trouble Signs	Controls
Leafhoppers	These yellow, brown, or green wedge-shape insects are less than ½ inch long. When you walk across a lawn, they flit away. They are especially active on East and West coasts, but can be found anywhere. They suck juices from leaves, causing grass to turn white, later yellow, then brown.	Control with Diazinon or carbaryl when leafhoppers are most abundant.
Mites	Clover mites show as tiny red specks against white paper. They are found in lawns across the country. Bermuda grass mites are pale green and microscopic; they may occur in Gulf Coast and western lawns. All spiderlike mites suck juices from grass leaves. Grass wilts, turns yellow, and dies.	Because overly succulent grass growth attracts mites, avoid heavy fertilization of your lawn. Control with Diazinon at first sign of infestation.
Mole crickets	These brownish insects are about 1½ inches long and mostly a problem in southern lawns. They cut off underground stems and roots in the day and work on stems at night, leaving lawns with areas that appear closely clipped. They like moist, warm weather.	Control with Diazinon.
Nematodes	Transparent roundworms with whitish or yellowish tint. They are tiny, often microscopic. Their presence may not be realized until a bleached-out area is apparent. The pests feed mainly on grass roots but some feed on stem and leaves. Disease may set in because of weakened turf.	To avoid and suppress nematodes, keep turf well-fed and water on schedule. Won't require chemical treatment.
Sod webworms	These tan-colored moths, about ¾ inch long, lay eggs at dusk. Gray or light brown larvae up to 1 inch long feed on bluegrasses and bent grasses, doing most damage from spring to midsummer. Feed on shoots and crowns of grass, causing irregular, close-clipped brown patches.	Treat with carbaryl or Diazinon when larvae are present.

GROUND COVERS

Ground covers are more than a type of plant. Low-growing and low-maintenance, these versatile gems are lifesavers in a landscape. Ground covers, which grow together to form a dense carpet for your outdoor living room, will thrive under trees and shrubs where other plants will not grow. Many bring color with flowers, foliage, or fruit. Ground covers also can unite elements of the landscape, making a transition between the wild and the tame, the lone and the mass, the newly planted and the mature. Use ground covers where you want a quick cover, to keep erosion to a minimum, or to carpet beds of flowering bulbs. Once planted, they'll grow happily without any pampering from you.

GROUND COVERS IN THE LANDSCAPE

Pachysandra (*right,* back) and ajuga (*right,* front) are two popular ground covers. They prosper in rich, moist soil in a shaded or partly sunny spot. Ajuga, or bugleweed, grows 4 to 6 inches tall and quickly forms a dense mat of green, bronze, or variegated foliage. Its flowers, which are usually blue (but also may be pink or white), appear in spring. Pachysandra is an evergreen plant that grows 6 to 8 inches high, with scalloped, shiny green leaves and tiny white blooms in the spring. Varieties also are available with green leaves edged in white.

Another good choice for moist, shaded areas is wintercreeper (*Euonymus fortunei*), which offers attractive foliage. It roots itself as it trails along the ground.

Deep shade won't hamper the spread of sweet woodruff (*Asperula odorata*). This delightful, low-growing ground cover (*right*) grows rapidly when tucked under and between trees and low shrubs. Only a few inches high, it produces delicate white flowers in spring over star-like leaves.

Good companion plants for sweet woodruff include one of the many hostas (back of photo, *right*), best known for their textured and variegated foliage; periwinkle (*Vinca minor*), which produce blue flowers in the spring; the hardy ivies, for their many leaf types and forms; silver-edged lamium, useful in problem spots; epimedium, which have heart-shaped leaves that hide tiny pink or yellow flowers; and ferns.

Shrublike ground covers, such as the heaths and heathers at *left*, offer soft textures and subtle colors with evergreen needles and pink, white, or red blossoms. Although heath (erica) blooms in spring and heather (calluna) blooms in the fall, both have similar care requirements. They need full sun to produce flowers, and an acidic, moist, very poor soil to thrive. Clip when overgrown and mulch well for winter.

Low-growing shrubs also make excellent ground covers. At the top of the list are cotoneasters, which bear tiny white flowers and bright berries. Other good shrub candidates include ground-hugging junipers, honeysuckle, jasmine, hypericum, broom, sarcococca, skimmia, bearberry, and holly.

When environmental factors such as heat, moisture, or soil pH limit your shrub choices, select a native ground cover that is better suited to your conditions. When you pick plants indigenous to your climate, they will grow better and you'll have less care. The California hillside pictured at *left* is planted with cacti, succulents, ice plant, pepper tree, statice, and palms—a perfect example of a nontraditional use of ground covers. Sedums and live-forevers also thrive in hot, dry spots.

If moist soils prevail, try bog andromeda, forget-me-not, or watercress (if you have running water nearby). Salty sea breezes won't bother thrift, pine, lamb's-ears, bearberry, and some ornamental grasses.

GALLERY OF GROUND COVERS

Aegopodium podagraria
Bishop's weed or goutweed

This ground cover grows 8 to 10 inches tall, with a profusion of green and white variegated leaves and a cluster of white flowers. It will thrive under almost any condition. However, it tends to be weedy and should be planted where the roots will be contained.

Ajuga reptans
Carpet bugle or bugleweed

Ajuga is happy in sun or shade and prefers a moist soil. Blue flower spikes rise 4 to 6 inches high over the foliage in mid-spring; rosettes of shiny green or bronze leaves lie flat on the ground. Ajuga is useful in self-contained borders around patios or front entrances.

BUTTERCUP
Ranunculus species

Buttercup covers a variety of plants, from those that are decorative to others that are more weedy. The flowers are yellow or white, appearing in mid-May over leaves and stems that creep along the ground. Some members of this family adapt well to rock gardens.

IVY
English ivy: *Hedera helix*
Boston ivy: *Parthenocissus tricuspidata*

Ivy grows rapidly over the ground, as well as on walls and fences. It is tolerant of shade and poor soil, but will thrive in a rich, moist soil. Boston ivy turns scarlet in the fall.

Lamium **species**
Dead nettle

Like other members of the mint family, lamium grows rapidly to fill in empty spaces. Leaves are silver and green; flowers are purple or yellow in spring. Lamium prefers partial shade and tends to get weedy.

LIRIOPE
Lilyturf

Evergreen in warm areas, liriope has grasslike leaves that are green or variegated and spikes of lilac-blue or white flowers that appear in fall. This tufted ground cover will grow equally well in sun or shade. Propagate by division.

EPIMEDIUM
Epimedium grandiflorum

This plant has wiry stems with heart-shape leaves that turn from light green to red in fall. Spring blooms are yellow or pink, forming underneath the foliage. Epimedium likes sun or partial shade. It is well suited to rock gardens, and will grow under trees.

Euonymus fortunei
Winter creeper

This ground cover belongs to a large family of shrubs and vines. Evergreen plants vary in color from green to purple. Rooting as it trails along, winter creeper is good on banks for erosion control. Use in full sun or light shade.

FERNS
Variety of genera and species

Grown from spores rather than seeds, ferns are best loved for their performance in deep shade and cool, woodland areas. An organic soil kept moist is best. Watch for delicate fronds that emerge from the ground in spring.

ORNAMENTAL GRASS
Variety of genera and species

Ornamental grasses are especially good for use in full sun or for slopes and dry, sandy locations. Tall plumes of pampas grass, graceful arches of fountain grass, or blue festucas add interest and color to any landscape.

Pachysandra terminalis
Japanese spurge

This plant is one of the most popular selections for carpeting the ground in a moist, shady area. Dark, evergreen leaves, 6 to 8 inches tall, are topped in the spring with small, white flowers. Spreads slowly, but worth waiting for.

Vinca minor
Periwinkle, creeping myrtle

Dark, shiny leaves are topped by a multitude of lavender flowers in mid-spring. An evergreen growing in sun in zones 4 to 7, or shade in all areas, vinca grows well in all but the poorest soil. Good for slopes. Vinca divides easily.

CHOOSING AND USING GROUND COVERS

Ground covers play a vital role in landscape design—it's hard to picture a perfect landscape without them. But when you plan your ground covers, you need to consider more than appearance. You must be sure you're choosing the right plant for the right spot, considering light, climate, moisture, soil, and use.

LANDSCAPE USES

■ Traditionally, ground covers are used to form a carpet under and between trees and shrubs where grasses have difficulty growing. Along with being aesthetically pleasing, ground covers also reduce weeds and conserve soil moisture for the trees and shrubs around them. Where only a few shrubs or trees appear in a simple landscape design, a complementary ground cover will tie the plants into a unit, serving as a base or a platform.

Ground covers are also good solutions for slopes or other spots where grasses will not grow, or would be difficult to maintain. A ground cover will add color and interest to these otherwise bare settings, and prevent erosion on steep grades. When you choose a ground cover for a hillside, select one with a heavy root system that will knit in with the soil. Good choices include ivy, hosta, daylilies, or ice plant.

Very low-growing plants, such as thrift, pearlwort, creeping thyme, sedum, and baby's-tears, work well as fillers between stepping-stones. These plants make a soft cushion that is aromatic when stepped on. You also can use ground covers to direct traffic away from an area. Or plant them in crevices of retaining walls to add color.

If pachysandra (*above*) is not held in bounds, it may encroach upon a lawn or path. Use brick or metal edgings to restrain growth.

SPECIAL FEATURES

■ Faced with a spot where nothing will grow? Many ground covers stand up to the most adverse growing conditions. Those types that tolerate poor soil and dry locations, for example, include foamflower, lamium, goutweed, crown vetch, and sedum. Where rocks and outcroppings create awkward-to-plant nooks and crags, you can fill in with rock cress, thrift, candytuft, Irish moss, pearlwort, and santolina.

Consider foliage in choosing ground covers. Many have unusual colors and add lovely highlights. Ground covers with bright foliage include bronze ajuga, blue festuca, silver snow-in-summer, or purple wintercreeper. Flowers, too, add needed color to the landscape design, from spring's gold alyssum and white candytuft to fall's purple liriope.

At least once a year (more often if necessary), trim euonymous (*above*) to encourage thicker growth and make a neater appearance.

When you need a ground cover in a spot near an open window or next to a deck, choose a fragrant plant such as lily-of-the-valley. Or for a double-duty cover-up, carpet your ground with an edible delight such as strawberries.

POST-PLANTING CARE

■ Whatever ground covers you select, they'll stay at their best if you follow a few basic maintenance steps. Plant ground covers in spring or fall and water until plants get established. Many drought-resistant varieties can go without watering, but even they do best when adequately watered. To prevent soil erosion, slowly apply water to slopes. Feed ground covers in early spring with a complete fertilizer, and mulch semihardy types in the fall in cold-winter areas.

1 When ground covers, such as the lamium *above,* become overcrowded, divide them and plant them elsewhere in your garden or share them with friends. Water well before lifting and pulling plants apart. Some tearing of roots is inevitable when you pull up the plants, but you can keep it to a minimum if you're careful.

Divide and replant ground covers in spring or fall. In the fall, leave enough time for roots to become established before the ground freezes. Plant ground covers at the same level they were growing before. Spacing depends on how quickly the plant grows and on your budget. If you set plants 6 inches apart, 100 plants will cover 25 square feet.

2 Lamium, a fast-growing cover plant, can be spaced farther apart than slow-growing types such as pachysandra and epimedium. Keep the area weed-free while plants are filling in.

3 Water well after planting until roots show new growth. Mulch to protect over the winter and to retain moisture in the spring. Obtain new plants from nurseries or mail-order catalogs.

VINES

Landscape improvement is a snap when you put a vine to work. These adaptable plants will grow anywhere, easily handling even tough assignments, like controlling erosion or providing privacy. Grow vines up and over arbors, trellises, fences, walls, and buildings. Or, let a vine become a blooming backdrop for a flower garden. For shady spots where lawn grasses fail, some vines will create a carpet of colorful flowers. In the front yard, plant these vining ground covers along a walk or foundation. Before you know it, you'll have a welcome mat of blooms. Read on for more information about these great garden helpers.

VINES IN THE LANDSCAPE

Vines offer inexpensive, practical solutions for hard-to-solve landscape problems in a yard. A large flowering vine like wisteria can be used to soften the sharp architectural lines of an exposed porch, deck, or patio. And, at the same time, the plant will add shade, privacy, and beauty to the setting. Smaller vines, such as clematis and plumbago, will easily disguise a porch pillar, stairway railing, arbor, or small shed. If you need to camouflage a fence or wall, vines like Dutchman's pipe, trumpet vine, star jasmine, and honeysuckle are hard to beat.

Place evergreen vines on the north side of your house, and deciduous vines on the south or west side. Evergreen types will insulate walls year-round; deciduous types will provide shade in the summer and let the sun into the house during the winter.

When you select a vine, consider its growth rate versus your available space. Consider also bloom time, color, fragrance, and foliage texture. Some vines will cling directly to the house; others need to be grown on a sturdy support, such as a trellis, arbor, or fence.

Use clematis (*above*) to perk up a wall with show-stopping blooms in May and June. Unlike many other vines, clematis is easy to control, rarely growing over 12 feet long.

The delicate fragrance and pastel blooms of the wisteria (*above*) have made it a favorite with gardeners across the country. A good choice for a porch or overhead structure, wisteria produces long clusters of blue, rose, or white flowers in May. Useful in the same way in warm climates is the exotic and bright bougainvillea (*opposite*). This vine looks terrific when trained around doors and windows.

A fence can be turned into a backdrop of green with a vine like honeysuckle (*above*). Without support, this versatile vine will carpet the ground to prevent erosion on steep slopes.

SHRUBS

Shrubs can be the most lovely, low-maintenance components of your landscape design. Though their beauty is subtle at times, shrubs give a landscape year-round continuity. They can act as natural privacy screens, fill a bare spot, soften the lines of your house's foundation, or be spotlighted alone.

There are as many evergreen and deciduous shrubs to choose from as there are uses for them. Although the blooms of a flowering shrub may be a good choice for some parts of your yard, consider a shrub's other features as well; after all, the shrub will spend most of the year without blooms. Keep in mind other seasonal rewards, such as autumn color, decorative fruit, and colorful bark.

SHRUBS IN THE LANDSCAPE

Shrubs can put the finishing touches on an existing planting scheme, serve as a first budget-minded purchase for a new home, or rejuvenate a tired landscape. Before making your selections, consider your special situation and the shrubs that will grow best in your climate.

TYPES OF SHRUBS

■ Shrubs fall into three general categories: (1) Narrow-leaved, or coniferous, evergreens, which keep their foliage year-round. Many are pyramidal in shape. Pines, yews, and junipers belong to this group. (2) Broad-leaved evergreens, including rhododendrons, hollies, boxwoods, and camellias. Some are evergreen only in the South. (3) Deciduous shrubs, which lose their leaves once a year. Many are flowering.

HOW TO SELECT SHRUBS

■ The shrubs you choose should blend with, not detract from, the style of your house. If you have a ranch-style house, for example, avoid shrubs that will grow up to block windows, and plants with severe upright forms that conflict with the house's horizontal lines.

To create a natural setting for your home, use shrubs to soften structural edges. Informal masses of evergreens at the corners of a two-story house, for example, will produce a lush frame around its foundation. For best effect, use shrubs with contrasting size and texture. The feathery foliage of juniper will enhance the looks of a shiny broad-leaved evergreen.

Although shrubs are usually planted in groups, some types can stand on their own. These specimens should have something special to offer, such as flowers, unique shape, or colorful foliage.

In the front yard *below,* a variety of evergreen shrubs and trees planted along the house and driveway add beauty and privacy. Consider the ultimate plant heights so your shrubs won't outgrow their setting.

For a showy, gracefully arching accent, try weigela (*right*). This deciduous shrub is tolerant of most soil types and prefers full sun or partial shade. Blossom colors are white, pink, red, and magenta.

SHRUBS IN THE LANDSCAPE

In southern gardens, few shrubs can compare with the bold and beautiful hibiscus. Growing to a height of 15 feet, this compact, hardy shrub looks best near an entryway, planted as a specimen, or mixed with lower-growing flowers. In the narrow bed at *right,* Agnes Galt hibiscus blooms with red- and pink-flowering snapdragons, petunias, and geraniums. Hibiscus grows best in a sunny location and is available in both red- and white-flowering varieties. Some hibiscus varieties are hardy in northern states.

Although full sun is best, the following shrubs will tolerate light shade: rhododendron, honeysuckle, hydrangea, aucuba, andromeda, mahonia, mountain laurel, winged euonymus, kerria, sweet pepperbush, and rose-of-Sharon.

The broad-leaved evergreens are the aristocrats of the evergreen family. Hardy only in areas where winter temperatures stay above zero, these shrubs have glossy green foliage that contrasts beautifully with their hardier needle-leaved cousins. Many species, including rhododendron, oleander, and andromeda, also produce dazzling flowers.

The lily-of-the-valley-like flowers of andromeda (*right*) appear every spring. You can use andromeda in a foundation planting or as a specimen plant. Andromeda prefers a moist, partially shady location with slightly acidic soil. Of the two most popular species, floribunda and japonica, the floribunda is slightly more hardy. Although it's slow growing, andromeda will eventually reach a height of 15 feet if left unpruned. If pruning is required, do it right after the flowers fade.

Use deciduous flowering shrubs as a colorful and less-demanding alternative to annual and perennial flowers. In just a few years, the lilacs at *left* transformed a bare, unsightly garden spot into a pocket of brilliance. One lavender- and one white-flowering variety mark the beginning of this border filled with hostas and coralbells.

The lilac's large, fragrant heads of single or double flowers make it a garden treasure during the months of May and June. This popular shrub grows to about 12 feet tall but can be pruned to any height to make a specimen plant or hedge. Available in shades of purple, blue, white, and pink, the lilac thrives in a sunny location with a slightly alkaline soil. Only dense shade prevents this hardy plant from blooming.

Because shrub borders are permanent landscape features, select shrubs that will provide interest year-round. Colorful berries, bark, and foliage will carry on the show long after spring blooms have faded. The low-growing *Viburnum plicatum* at *left* has showy, maplelike leaves and produces crownlike heads of small white flowers in May. In fall, its leaves turn scarlet, and red berries hang from the plant's branches even after the leaves have fallen off.

Other shrubs that provide brilliant fall foliage color include sumac, rhododendron, crape myrtle, and mahonia. For berries, try pyracantha, cotoneaster, holly, quince, chokeberry, bayberry, barberry, and mahonia. Shrubs with beautiful bare branches for winter landscapes include red-osier dogwood, chokeberry, kerria, crape myrtle, witch hazel, and sumac.

HOW TO PLANT A SHRUB

Spring and fall are the best times to plant new shrubs. Many gardeners prefer fall planting, because shrub roots will grow well into winter, giving the plant a head start on top growth the following spring.

The old adage about not putting a $10 plant in a 10-cent hole still holds true, and it's one to be adhered to if you want shrubs to perform in your landscape. Before digging a hole, consider your shrub's needs, including sunlight, soil conditions, pruning requirements, and winter protection.

SOIL PREPARATION
■ Loose, fertile soil will provide adequate drainage and aeration, and retain water and nutrients to sustain plant growth. For proper soil preparation, see *pages 8–9*. Before planting, test your soil for its pH level. Most shrubs require a neutral pH (between 6 and 7). If you have a low (too acidic) pH, add a phosphorus source, such as superphosphate or lime. Some broad-leaved evergreens, such as rhododendrons and azaleas, prefer an acidic soil. If your soil's pH is too high, you can lower it by mixing in sulfur or iron sulfate.

TYPES OF SHRUB STOCK
■ Shrubs are sold in one of three ways: bare root, the type usually sold by mail-order nurseries; balled-and-burlapped (B&B), almost always an evergreen which is field grown, dug with a ball of soil around its roots, and wrapped in burlap; and container grown, most often used for deciduous stock.

Timing is important when planting shrubs. Bare-root or deciduous shrubs should be planted when they're dormant, either in early spring before growth starts or in late fall after it has stopped. Container and balled-and-burlapped plants are most successfully planted when temperatures are cool and root growth is at its height, but they can be planted at any time the soil is workable. In the summer, give extra attention to watering.

BARE-ROOT SHRUBS
■ Bare-root shrubs should be planted as soon as possible. If planting is delayed, keep roots cool and moist by wrapping them in dampened peat moss or newspaper. To plant the shrub, dig a hole that will accommodate all of the shrub's roots. Never crowd the roots or jam

Remove containers by turning them upside down and tapping them gently or by cutting them away with shears. If roots are encircled around the ball, be sure to loosen them before planting.

When you plant B&B shrubs, set the plant at the same level it grew before. Remove any wires or cords. Pull the burlap slightly away from the ball, but do not remove it; it will disintegrate in time.

them into the bottom of a hole that's too small. After digging the hole, mold a loose cone of soil in the bottom. Set the shrub on top of the cone and spread the roots over it. Holding the shrub in an upright position, fill the planting hole about two-thirds full. Gently tamp down the soil around the roots and fill the hole with water. After the water has drained, fill with soil.

BALLED-AND-BURLAPPED AND CONTAINER SHRUBS

■ Balled-and-burlapped and container-grown shrubs are more expensive than bare-root plants. Because they're already growing in their root balls, however, they'll adjust more quickly to transplanting and start growing much

faster. Both of these types must be kept well watered until planted. At planting time, dig a hole larger than the root ball. Set the shrub into the hole at the same level it grew before. Loosen the burlap only at the trunk. (The burlap will decay rapidly and will not interfere with root development.) If the root ball is wrapped in a plastic or cardboard container, carefully cut away the covering after the shrub is positioned in the hole. Backfill the hole as you would with a bare-root shrub.

POST-PLANTING CARE

■ To help a deciduous shrub adjust to the shock of transplanting, remove about one-third of the branches. Pruning will compensate for any possible

root loss during the move. Start by cutting out broken branches and young shoots sprouting low on the plant. Then cut away the weaker branch of any V-shaped crotch. Shear evergreens only to make the shape of the plant uniform.

Top priority should be given to watering newly planted shrubs. Dig a shallow trough around the root area to catch water. If rainfall is low the first season, saturate the soil at least once a week with a light trickle from a garden hose, or use a soaker hose.

Mulch will help conserve moisture, ward off weeds, and keep soil insulated in the winter. Place a 3- to 4-inch layer of straw, wood chips, or leaves beneath the spread of branches to within an inch or two of the trunk.

HEDGES

Hedges can be used to define a lot line, screen an unsightly view, beautify a foundation, or add privacy. An informal hedge is most often used as a screen or in a naturalized setting and requires little or no pruning. A formal hedge requires periodic pruning and usually serves as a property divider or border.

Good shrubs to use in an informal hedge include spirea, lilac, forsythia, honeysuckle, hydrangea, and ninebark. The bridal wreath spirea, *Spirea vanhouttei*, at *right* has been popular since the beginning of the century. An extra-hardy species, spirea grows to 7 feet tall if left unpruned, but is easily pruned to any height. In May, its long, graceful branches produce thousands of fragrant small white flowers, and in the fall, the foliage turns bright orange.

Almost any plant can be used as a hedge, but for best results, choose one with a uniform growth habit, heavy branching, and dense foliage. Tall, blooming shrubs, such as the forsythia at *right,* can add a wall of color where a landscape needs it most. Often used to define property lines, a row of forsythia also can make a smashing backdrop for a border of low-growing shrubs, bulbs, or flowers. Buttercup yellow flowers grace its branches in early spring. In the far North, where winters are cold, forsythia does not bloom reliably.

A shorter hedge can create an effective lot-line barrier without blocking the view. Thorny shrubs, such as barberry, shrub polyantha, and species rose, will discourage animals and people from cutting through your hedge.

The type of shrubs you plant and the way you prune them should depend on the size and style of the rest of your landscape. Deciduous flowering shrubs are custom-made for a natural, low-maintenance landscape plan. Fast growing and almost care-free, the honeysuckle hedge at *left* grows to 8 feet tall if left unpruned. These hardy shrubs aren't particular about soil type, and they have few insect or disease problems. Set plants at least half their mature width from property lines to avoid overgrowth later on.

Formal hedges take up less space than informal hedges, making them ideal for small lots. If you prefer a formal look, plant privet, box, barberry, or Tallhedge. All of these plants can easily be pruned to any height or shape.

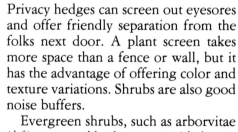

Privacy hedges can screen out eyesores and offer friendly separation from the folks next door. A plant screen takes more space than a fence or wall, but it has the advantage of offering color and texture variations. Shrubs are also good noise buffers.

Evergreen shrubs, such as arborvitae (*left*), yew, and barberry, provide better year-round privacy than the deciduous types because they keep their foliage in the winter. However, deciduous shrubs grow faster than evergreens. Popular deciduous screens include lilac, privet, Tallhedge, winged euonymus, spirea, viburnum, honeysuckle, and forsythia. Whether you select an evergreen or deciduous hedge, choose shrubs that will grow densely. For tight spaces, pick an upright, columnar type rather than one with a broad base.

63

CARE AND MAINTENANCE

Shrubs are among the easiest plants to care for. Except for pruning, you'll need to spend a minimal amount of time to keep them at their best.

FERTILIZING

■ Evergreen shrubs will grow without fertilizing, but deciduous shrubs benefit from a supplementary feeding once a year. The best times to feed are early spring or late fall after the plants have gone dormant. Fertilizing in late fall is often more beneficial because it allows the roots to take up nutrients in the very early spring when root growth starts. Don't feed shrubs in late summer or early fall, because feeding stimulates new growth that will not have time to harden off before winter's cold.

Use a complete fertilizer containing 5 to 12 percent nitrogen. For flowering shrubs, a fertilizer rich in phosphorus (such as 5-10-5) is best. Feed nonflowering shrubs at the same time you feed the lawn, with the same fertilizer.

Apply fertilizer evenly to the soil area as far as the branches reach to cover the entire root zone; water well. A supplementary liquid fertilizer applied to the foliage and soil will give an extra boost. To avoid burning the leaves, do not spray them on hot, sunny days.

Broad-leaved evergreens, such as azalea, rhododendron, camellia, laurel, and leucothoe, require an acidic soil to keep growing and blooming. For best results, dust annually with cottonseed meal or a special rhododendron-azalea-camellia fertilizer.

WATERING AND WEEDING

■ Watering and weeding are the two essentials for shrub survival, especially for young plants. Mulch will help re-

duce many of the time-consuming maintenance chores by keeping the ground cool, moist, and weed free. Do not lay mulch all the way to the shrub's stems; direct contact can cause stem rot, and organic material makes attractive nesting sites for small animals who may make a meal of your shrubs. During periods of hot, dry weather, water shrubs deeply on a weekly basis.

INSECTS AND DISEASES

■ Unfortunately, some insects and diseases like your shrubs as much as you do. For insurance against insect invasions, use a dormant oil spray on flowering shrubs in early spring before buds break. Such sprays can control scales, and often aphids and mites, on a variety of evergreen and deciduous plants. If your shrubs still show signs of stress, consult your local nurseryman.

Shrubs used as hedges should be cut back regularly to keep them in shape. Prune the bottom of the hedge wider than the top so the sun will fall on bottom branches and keep them full and dense.

Use the proper tools when caring for your shrubs. Sharp pruning shears should be used to head back evergreens or to train shrubs into special topiary or espalier shapes.

Use shears designed for each pruning job. Hedge clippers work well on thin or soft stems. For stems thicker than the center of pruning shears, use loppers or saw.

To increase next year's bloom on lilacs and rhododendrons, cut off this year's flower heads after blooming. Don't remove blossoms from fall berry producers.

Some shrubs, like forsythia, send out long arching branches. These can be rooted to form a new plant. Draw the stem to the ground and peg it down (*left*) with a clip to hold it in place until it roots.

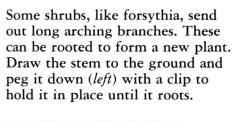

WINTER PROTECTION

■ In cold-winter areas, protect marginally hardy deciduous plants with a thick mulch of leaves, evergreen boughs, or wood chips after frost. Remove the mulch in spring. Because evergreens retain their foliage, they are vulnerable to drying winter winds. Watering all evergreen shrubs deeply before the ground freezes will help. To provide further protection, set up a four-sided burlap screen, and fill the area between the screen and plant with leaves or straw. If snow or ice coats branches, remove it to prevent breakage.

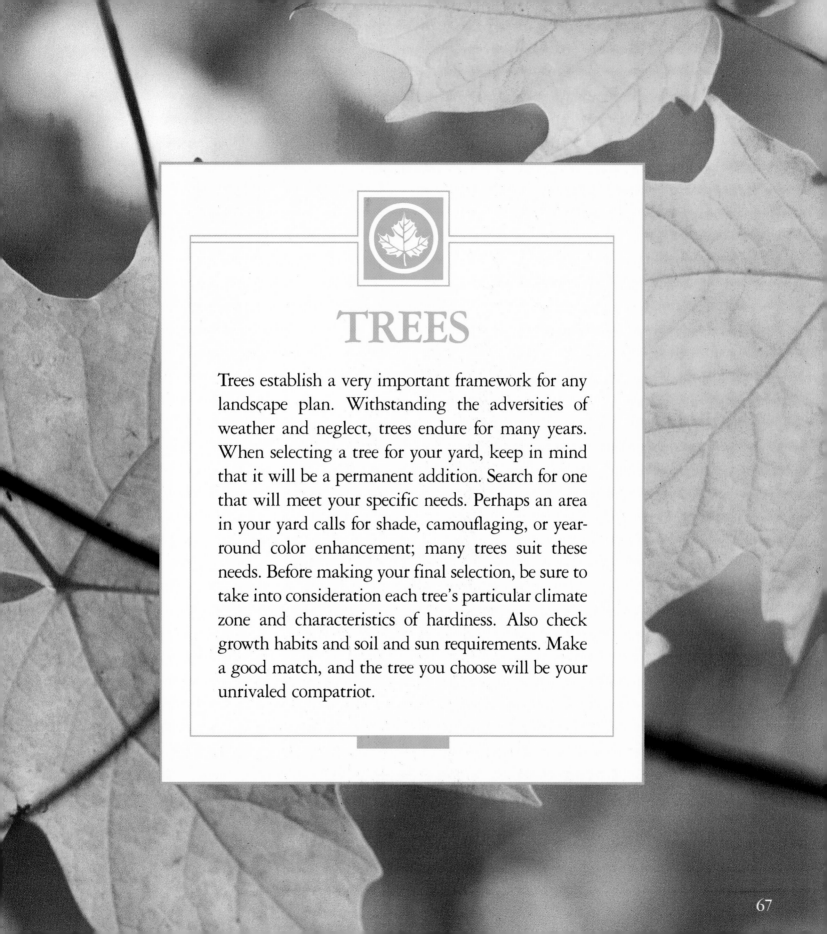

TREES

Trees establish a very important framework for any landscape plan. Withstanding the adversities of weather and neglect, trees endure for many years. When selecting a tree for your yard, keep in mind that it will be a permanent addition. Search for one that will meet your specific needs. Perhaps an area in your yard calls for shade, camouflaging, or year-round color enhancement; many trees suit these needs. Before making your final selection, be sure to take into consideration each tree's particular climate zone and characteristics of hardiness. Also check growth habits and soil and sun requirements. Make a good match, and the tree you choose will be your unrivaled compatriot.

TREES IN THE LANDSCAPE

Before you select a new tree, consider these variables: the mature height, which needs to be in proportion to the surroundings; the shape, which can be columnar, globular, or horizontal; and its intended use, such as screening, shade, or flowers. Evergreen trees will work best for screens or windbreaks; deciduous trees offer the advantages of bright autumn foliage color.

If you're still uncertain about what type of tree to plant, let the size and style of your house decide for you. Towering shade trees blend well with big homes on large lots. The stately old oak *opposite* protects this house from the elements. In the summer, its leafy shade helps keep down the temperature indoors. In the winter, its bare branches let the warm sunshine through.

Small trees work well on pocket-size lots. Appearing each spring as a cloud of white, the fragrant blossoms of the cherry tree *below* make a delightful contrast against the deep red leaves of Japanese maple. Other good choices are dogwood, redbud, flowering crab, star magnolia, and amur maple.

TREES IN THE LANDSCAPE

Consider the seasonal qualities of trees before you make your final selections. You can create an attractive all-season landscape by choosing a variety of shade and ornamental trees with different appealing qualities.

SPRING BLOOM

■ You know it's spring when certain ornamental trees burst into bloom. Favorite spring-blooming trees are redbud, dogwood, pear, flowering crab, acacia, horse chestnut, hawthorn, and tulip tree. Fruit trees, including apple, peach, cherry, and plum, will add their own colorful charm.

SUMMER BLOOM

■ Long, hot days can be brightened with a selection of summer-flowering trees. Crape myrtle, golden-rain tree, golden-chain tree, stewartia, silk tree, Japanese tree lilac, and catalpa are popular species in this category.

FALL FOLIAGE AND BERRIES

■ Many trees have breathtaking autumn leaf color. If yellow and gold are your favorite fall hues, choose ash, beech, birch, butternut, ginkgo, hickory, honey locust, linden, sugar maple, pecan, poplar, tulip tree, and walnut. If you prefer red tones, pick dogwood; hawthorn; sophora; red maple; pin, red, and scarlet oak; sour gum; sourwood; and sweet gum. Bright orange foliage graces yellowwood, Ohio buckeye, and paperbark maple. The sourwood (sorrel tree) blooms in fall at the same time that its foliage turns red.

Fall also is a time for fruits and berries. These often hang on well into winter and provide color against a snowy landscape. To add fruits and berries to your landscape, select trees such as dogwood, hawthorn, Russian olive, holly, flowering crab, sourwood, golden-rain tree, and mountain ash.

WINTER INTEREST

■ The pageantry of trees doesn't have to close down for the season when winter arrives. You can add interest to an otherwise dreary landscape with colorful or patterned bark or an unusual trunk shape. Beautiful bark is found on crape myrtle, birch, beech, sweet gum, sycamore, willow, cherry, and eucalyptus. Trees with attractive silhouettes include weeping cherry or birch, crape myrtle, katsura tree, dogwood, magnolia, poplar, zelkova, and tulip tree. Evergreens add color to a snowy yard by keeping their foliage year-round.

ALL-SEASON INTEREST

■ Many trees will give you the best of all worlds by offering color and interest every season through flowers, foliage, fruit, and bark. The dogwoods *below* display white flowers in spring, scarlet leaves in fall, and wine-colored berries in winter to make a striking year-round accent. Other top choices are sweet gum, crape myrtle, sourwood, hawthorn, holly, and pear.

Trees that bear fruit or nuts are a natural source of food for wildlife. To attract winged and four-legged creatures to your yard, plant such trees as red and white oak, red maple, white pine, hemlock, birch, Russian olive, amur maple, blue and Norway spruce, beech, red cedar, serviceberry, mountain ash, hawthorn, dogwood, flowering crab, hackberry, and mulberry.

Small trees are ideal for small lots because they won't interfere with other gardening. The redbud at *left* works exceedingly well as an accent in a bulb border; redbud's canopy of leaves will appear after the blossoms of the sun-loving tulips and daffodils have faded.

Many people thrive on city life, but some tree species can't adjust to the soot and grime of the urban environment. Shade trees that have proved to be tolerant to air pollution include Norway maple, honey locust, little-leaved linden (it is sensitive to salt compounds—don't plant it along a street or walkway that might be salted during the winter), ginkgo, pin oak, Austrian pine, willow, horse chestnut, hackberry, and ash.

Choose a tall, columnar evergreen if you want to soften a wall or hide an eyesore. The pyramidal Chinese junipers planted in the narrow strip between driveways at *left* offer both privacy and a refreshing break from an otherwise humdrum landscape plan. A mulch of chipped bark keeps weeding and watering to a minimum.

Keep evergreens pruned to retain an appropriate shape and size for their location in your landscape. Once oddly shaped and overgrown, evergreens usually are hard to restore.

Other plants that can be used for effective privacy screening include poplar, hemlock, arborvitae, podocarpus, and cypress. Fir, cedar, pine, juniper, holly, false cypress, and eucalyptus are equally attractive when planted close together to act as a tall hedge.

71

GALLERY OF TREES

BIRCH
Betula species

Birches are a group of attractive, relatively short-lived trees used for their decorative qualities. The bark of the paper or canoe (*B. papyrifera*), weeping (*B. pendula*), and gray (*B. populifolia*) birches is white; the bark of the river birch (*B. nigra*) is chocolate brown.

SOIL: River birch: wet; canoe and other birches: prefer moist soil, but tolerate other soils

LIGHT: Full sun to light shade

HARDINESS: Zone 2 to 4

COMMENTS: The river and canoe birches are the largest growing, reaching up to 90 feet tall. Weeping birch is next in size, reaching up to 50 feet high. The gray birch is the smallest at about 25 feet tall. The canoe birch grows in clumps of two to four trunks; the weeping birch has the characteristic pendulous branches.

CRAB APPLE
Malus species and hybrids

Crab apples are showy, small trees with white, pink, or red single, semidouble, or double flowers in mid-spring. Decorative and edible red, yellow, or green fruit forms in early fall. Fruit is bitter but can be used in jams or jellies. Crab apples reach 15 to 25 feet in height and have a wide spread.

SOIL: Rich, well drained; tolerates acid, alkaline, or wet

LIGHT: Full sun

HARDINESS: Zone 3 to 5

COMMENTS: It's common to have crab apples bloom profusely one year and then not bloom well the next. Good choices include: the white Japanese crab apple (*M. floribunda*); the red Hopa; the pink tea (*M. hupehensis*); the white Sargent (*M. sargenti*); and the Red Jade with white flowers and bright red berries on weeping branches.

DOGWOOD
Cornus species

Dogwoods are showy, highly prized for landscaping, and valued for their size, shape, flowers, fall foliage, and bright berries. The two major tree species are the flowering dogwood (*C. florida*) and the Japanese dogwood (*C. kousa*). Flowers are white or pink, with four rounded petals in mid-spring. The Japanese dogwood blooms about a month later, with larger, pointed, white flowers. Both reach about 20 feet in height, and produce architecturally interesting, horizontal branches.

SOIL: Rich, well drained, slightly acidic, moist. Add magnesium for bloom.

LIGHT: Full sun to part shade

HARDINESS: Flowering, Zone 5 Japanese, Zone 6

COMMENTS: Buds form in fall with the berries and scarlet leaves. The best spring flowers follow hot, dry falls.

GINKGO
Ginkgo biloba

This tree—also known as the maidenhair tree—is tough and attractive, especially in fall, with its golden foliage. The leaves are fan-shape, like those on the maidenhair fern. Trees can reach 75 feet high but usually do not grow taller than 50 feet. This slow grower is an excellent lawn or street tree because of its high tolerance of pollution. Young trees have an awkward shape. Plant only male trees, as the female has a fruit with an unpleasant odor.

SOIL: Deep, loose, well drained. Water heavily after planting.
LIGHT: Full sun to part shade
HARDINESS: Zone 5
COMMENTS: Ginkgo has always been rated as one of the best urban or city trees. It is relatively pest-free. In the fall, all the leaves drop at the same time, making raking easier.

GOLDEN-CHAIN TREE
Laburnum species

The golden-chain tree is best known for the long—12- to 18-inch—clusters of yellow, pealike flowers in mid-spring that resemble wisteria blossoms. After blooming, the tree has little interest and no fall color. The mature height of the golden-chain tree is about 30 feet. The leaves are bright green and cloverlike on branches that generally grow upright but sometimes develop into a shrubby form. There are two available types: the common golden-chain (*L. anagyroides*) and a hybrid (*L. x watereri*), which many gardeners claim as the better of the two.

SOIL: Well drained, moist, acidic
LIGHT: Full sun to light shade. Do not use in hot afternoon sun.
HARDINESS: Zone 6
COMMENTS: Frequent pruning might be needed to keep plants in shape. The seedpods, which form in the fall and cling until midwinter, are poisonous.

HAWTHORN
Crataegus species

Hawthorns are small and decorative trees, reaching about 25 feet in height and spreading up to 20 feet wide. They are known for their late-spring white or pink flowers and bright red or scarlet berries—the berries may remain on the limbs all winter. All hawthorns except the English turn bronze or orange in fall. The plants have stiff thorns along the branches.

SOIL: Prefer poor, dry soils.
LIGHT: Full sun or light shade
HARDINESS: Zone 5
COMMENTS: Many excellent hawthorns are available. Their major problem is a susceptibility to fire blight. Choose between the cockspur (*C. crusgalli*), Lavalle (*C. x lavallei*), English (*C. oxyacantha*), or Washington (*C. phaenopyrum*). Good hybrids include Autumn Glory, Toba, Winter King, or Paulii (Paul's Scarlet), a variety that does not form fruits.

How to Plant a Tree

Trees can be planted any time the ground can be worked, but spring or fall are the best times to plant most types. If you plant in summer, you'll have to water more frequently. Spring planting is recommended for the rain tree, tulip tree, magnolia, black gum, and several oaks (red, scarlet, English, bur, willow, and white), which should not be moved in fall.

PLACEMENT

■ Because most trees need sun, plant a new specimen where it will not be shaded by buildings or larger trees. Consider the tree's mature size and shape, and don't locate it where it will eventually grow into other plants or your home.

Large shade trees with wide-spreading branches—such as oak, maple, linden, and elm—need at least 65 feet between their trunks. Plant them 30 feet from your house and 10 feet from walks, driveways, and patios so roots will not encroach upon and crack paved foundations. Columnar trees—such as gray birch, white poplar, and Lombardy poplar—can be planted closer together. Place small trees about 10 feet apart and at least 8 feet from your house.

SOIL PREPARATION

■ Although trees vary in their soil preferences, most do best in well-drained soils. To improve soil, till or spade in organic matter and a source of phosphorus, such as superphosphate. Do not fertilize again for at least another year.

Look also at the existing grade or soil level. If it needs to be raised, do so before planting. Grade changes made after a tree starts to grow can smother the roots and eventually damage or even kill the tree.

1 To plant balled-and-burlapped stock, first dig a hole twice as wide and at least 1½ times as deep as the root ball of the tree. This will allow for future root growth and avoid root damage.

TYPES OF TREE STOCK

■ Trees are sold as bare root, balled-and-burlapped, or containerized. Planting instructions for trees that are balled-and-burlapped are outlined in steps 1 through 6 on the *opposite* page. Follow the same steps for containerized material, but remove the container before planting. For all types, if you must delay planting time, keep the tree in a cool, shaded area, and water well until it can be set into the ground.

Plant bare-root trees in spring or fall when they are dormant. Keep the roots moist until planting, and soak roots in a bucket of water for 24 hours before planting. Form a cone of improved soil in the bottom of the planting hole and spread roots evenly over the cone. Remove broken or damaged roots and shorten too-long roots that would end up encircling the hole and competing with neighboring roots. Then follow steps 4 through 6 as outlined *opposite* for planting balled-and-burlapped trees.

POST-PLANTING CARE

■ Prune a newly planted tree to compensate for any root loss, and to shape the tree for future growth. For pruning instructions, see pages 80 and 81.

Newly planted trees should be staked to give them strength against high winds. Trees under 1 inch across

2 Place improved soil into the bottom of the hole so that the top of the ball will be level with the ground. Position the tree so its best side faces forward.

3 Cut the cord holding the ball and gently pull back, but do not remove, the burlap. That way, the root ball will not be disturbed. In time, the burlap will disintegrate.

4 Backfill the planting hole with improved soil until it is about half full, and water again. Tamp down the soil, holding the tree in a straight, upright position.

do not require staking. For trees with trunks between 1 and 3 inches across, use two stakes; trunks over 3 inches thick need support from three evenly placed stakes. Stakes should be tall enough to secure the tree just below the spot where the major branches split away from the trunk. Tie trees with heavy cord to prevent injury to bark. Don't wrap wire directly around bark.

Young trees, clad only in thin bark, are susceptible to sunscald. This malady occurs when the bark of the tree is warmed during the day by the winter sun, then is suddenly subjected to freezing temperatures at night. This condition often weakens trees. To prevent sunscald, wrap trees with a long strip of burlap or tree tape. Keep this protection in place until the tree develops the thick bark that mature trees have.

5 Fill the planting hole with water and allow it to drain. This will eliminate air pockets and ensure that roots will be in contact with soil particles.

6 After the water has drained, fill the planting hole to the top with improved soil. Make a catch basin for water by creating a raised circle of soil 2 to 3 inches high about a foot away from the tree.

CARE AND MAINTENANCE

Keep your prized shade trees healthy by paying attention to fertilizing, watering, winter protection, and insect and disease control.

FEEDING METHODS

■ Large trees should be fed every 3 to 4 years. Feeding in early spring or late fall is preferable; use a complete fertilizer such as 10-6-4 for trees that do not flower, or 5-10-5 for the ones that do.

To feed trees, either broadcast fertilizer on the soil surface, or inject it directly into the root zone. Trees in a lawn area can be surface-fed by applying fertilizer at a distance of 2½ feet from the trunk to 2 to 3 feet beyond the spread of the tree's branches. Use 10-6-4 at a rate of 1 pound per inch of trunk diameter for trees 3 inches across or less, and 3 pounds per inch of trunk diameter for trees over 3 inches across.

You can use a crow bar or a root feeder to make holes for feeding. For either method, fertilizer should be applied at least 2 feet from the base of the trunk. Feeder roots of younger trees are just inside the drip line (at the farthest tip of branches), and those of mature trees are outside the drip line.

For the crowbar method, make holes with a crowbar or auger at the rate of 10 to 15 for each inch of trunk diameter; space holes evenly around the perimeter of the drip line. Feed at the rate of 3 to 4 pounds of fertilizer per inch of trunk diameter if the tree's diameter is more than 6 inches, and 2 to 3 pounds per inch of diameter if it's less than 6 inches. Mix fertilizer with soil and pour into hole; do not use more than one cup of fertilizer per hole. Water well.

To make the feeding process even easier, use a root feeder (*right*). Simply fill the chamber with a compressed plant food cartridge, attach a garden hose to the feeder, and turn on the water. These feeders can also be used for deep-watering tree roots during periods of drought in the summer.

WATERING

■ Evergreens need special attention before cold weather settles in. Because these plants retain their foliage, they're very vulnerable to drying winter winds. Those on the south and west sides of your house will be the first to suffer. Unless you've had an especially wet fall, water all evergreens deeply before the ground freezes.

DISEASE AND INSECTS

■ Be on the lookout for signs of insects and diseases and treat them immediately. A dormant oil spray applied just before buds break will control many insect problems; do not apply dormant oil to sensitive plants such as sugar and Japanese maple, beech, hickory, walnut, butternut, Atlantic cedar, blue spruce, or Douglas fir.

INJURY REPAIR

■ If a large piece of bark is knocked off, nail it back before it dries out and cover the area with damp peat moss held in place with plastic, until the bark regrows. Or cut away the damaged bark and shape the wound into an oval with a sharp knife. Cover the area with a tree wound paint and inspect regularly. If the paint breaks or wears away, reapply.

Trees that have been damaged by the wind can usually be repaired. If young trees start to tilt from heavy winds, bring them back to their normal upright position and hold in place with wires or stakes until they strengthen and start to grow on their own. Uprooted trees may be saved if they are immediately righted and staked. Compensate for root loss by thinning out branches or pruning back.

Prune evergreens to maintain a pleasing, natural shape. This upright juniper should be trimmed back with hedge clippers to keep its pyramidal form.

This pine should be encouraged to retain a rounder shape. To keep branches compact and dense, cut the new growth (called a candle) back about half-way each spring.

Apply a sturdy plastic tree wrap to young trees to prevent damage to the bark from mowers and animals. This type of wrap is especially good for preventing rabbits from making a meal of your young trees.

Wrapping young trees can prevent sunscalding. In the fall, tie a tree wrap from the bottom up so there will be no lip that can collect water and cause fungus cankers to develop on the trunk.

Sometimes a leader will fail to grow or will break off. Select a shoot to be the new leader, and cut the surrounding ones back. If necessary, guide the leader into an upright position with a small stake.

ANNUALS

Annual flowers will grace your garden with instant beauty and color. By definition, an annual is a plant that grows, flowers, sets seed for its future generations, and dies in the same year. The term "annual" has also come to be applied to delicate perennials that will survive only mild winters. For gardeners and observers alike, the term "annual" has one more meaning: a myriad of color, size, form, and beauty that bursts forth in the garden from spring to fall. Whether the mood you want in your garden is quaint or sophisticated, bold or soft, you'll find an annual to fit any need. Every year you can anticipate a fresh new look, attained quickly, easily, and with minimal cost.

ANNUALS IN THE LANDSCAPE

Large or small, formal or informal, bold or subdued—whatever your landscape style, annuals can fit pleasantly into the plan. While perennials and bulbs go in and out of bloom, annuals provide the flower garden with season-long color and continuity.

As you design your garden, keep in mind that bright, exciting colors make the garden appear smaller than it actually is. Cool tones, which are more soothing to the eye, will make your garden seem larger. The mixed spring border *below* pops with bright, warm tones of red, yellow, and orange.

If you like a vivid color scheme, try marigolds, salvia, snapdragons, or celo-sia. For subtler tones, select the blues and violets of pansies, ageratums, or lobelias for a cooler, more tranquil effect. In any flower combination, choose complementary hues for an eye-pleasing canvas of color.

The mixture of Shirley poppies, annual chrysanthemums, and California poppies at *right* gives an informal, country look to this suburban garden. Cosmos and spider flower, with an edging of sweet alyssum, would also look lovely. If you'd like a more formal look, stick with beds of one variety of annual. Good choices include geraniums, marigolds, and petunias. For contrast, add a silvery dusty-miller edging.

SOWING SEEDS OUTDOORS

It's more economical to sow seeds outdoors than to plant purchased bedding plants, and seed racks give you a wider selection of varieties to choose from. Seeds won't give you instant results, however, and your success will be more dependent on Mother Nature. Whichever method you use, select varieties carefully by studying catalogs and seed packets. Different varieties offer different colors, heights, and resistance to weather, insects, and disease.

Timing is critical for sowing seeds outdoors. Some annuals are called "cool-season" types, and may be sown as early in spring as the soil can be worked. Wait to plant "warm-season" annuals until the chance of frost is past.

While some smaller annual seeds must be started indoors, the following can be started from seed sown directly in the garden:

- African daisy*
- Amaranthus
- Aster
- Calendula*
- California poppy*
- Candytuft
- Cape daisy
- Carnation
- Celosia
- Cleome
- Coreopsis
- Cornflower
- Cosmos
- Dahlia
- Dusty-miller
- Gaillardia
- Kochia
- Larkspur*
- Marigold
- Nasturtium
- Nemesia*
- Nierembergia
- Nigella*
- Phlox*
- Portulaca
- Scabiosa
- Stocks*
- Sweet alyssum*
- Sweet pea*
- Tithonia
- Zinnia

*Cool-season annual

Avoid the temptation to work soil too early. Wet soil will harden when it dries, preventing good root growth. To test for readiness, take a handful of soil and squeeze it; if it stays together, the soil is too wet for you to work. Wait a few days and try the test again.

When it's time to sow your seeds, pay particular attention to planting depth. If seeds are planted too shallow, they will dry out and not germinate. But if seeds are planted too deep, the soil may be too cold, may lack oxygen, or may present too much of a barrier for seeds to push through. A good rule is to plant seeds as deep as they are thick.

Some fine seeds, usually grown indoors, can be sown outdoors with the help of seed pellets or seed tapes, which you cut and lay on the ground.

Space most annuals a distance apart that is half of their mature height. Read seed packets for recommendations. Follow the spacing guidelines given below in inches for these annuals:

- African daisy 10–12
- Ageratum 6–8
- Aster 12–15
- Begonia 7–9
- Cleome 12–24
- Coleus 10–18
- Marigold 6–15
- Nasturtium 8–12
- Oriental pepper 6–8
- Pansy 4–6
- Petunia 12–14
- Salvia 6–8
- Snapdragon 6–8
- Sweet alyssum 6
- Sweet pea 10–12
- Zinnia 6–12

1 Good soil preparation is the key to a thriving, colorful annual garden. If you have a tiller, you can eliminate hand-spading and till the garden to a depth of 8 to 10 inches. Run the tiller across the first rows to break up soil even more. This method works well when starting a new flower bed.

3 Lay pieces of cord or clothesline on the ground to outline a design within the flower bed. Sow seeds evenly over the ground; cover slightly with soil. Keep moist by watering with a gentle spray from a sprinkler or hose, until strong growth appears.

2 Prepare the seedbed by incorporating organic material such as peat moss, compost, or manure; perlite or vermiculite for added porosity; and fertilizer. Work material in, apply water, and rake smooth; seeds will not germinate and grow in compacted, lumpy, or dry soil.

4 After the seedlings have developed two to three sets of leaves, you'll need to thin them. Carefully remove seedlings so that you don't disturb the others. Leave space between plants, as outlined on the chart on the previous page. After thinning, remove the cords you used to define the area.

5 Thinning allows your plants to grow to their ultimate size and shape. In a short time, your garden will look like the warm array of colors from the cosmos, zinnias, and marigolds pictured *above*.

If you remove the thinnings carefully, you can transplant them to another part of the garden or give them to friends. Label each plant so you'll remember what it is. To help you make choices for next season, record the varieties you've planted and how well they've performed for you.

STARTING ANNUALS FROM TRANSPLANTS

Bedding plants are right for you if you want an instant garden of beautiful blooms, or if you don't have the time, space, or inclination to start your own annuals from seed. Started flats and packs of almost any type of flowering annual can be purchased at local garden centers. Most of these plants should be planted after the last frost in your area. These transplants can give you a jump on summer color and transform your flower beds almost overnight from dull to sensational.

You'll get a lot of enjoyment from your annual investment in bedding plants. Professionally grown, they will be larger and easier to handle, will give you at least an extra month of color, and will be better established before midsummer's heat and drought have a chance to wilt and kill them.

1 When you shop for bedding plants, look for compact, bright green, healthy plants. The label will tell you about variety, color, and height. Don't reject those that aren't in bloom; all-green plants often do better in the long run.

2 If you can't plant right away, keep your new flowers moist. Remove the plants from the pack by holding them with one hand while inverting the pack. If they don't fall out easily, tap the bottom with a trowel.

3 If the plants are not in individual cells, separate them gently by hand or with a knife just before planting; don't allow roots to dry out. Soil in the planting bed should be tilled, enriched, and watered before planting.

4 If roots seem compacted, loosen them gently before planting. Dig a hole slightly larger than the root ball, and set the plant in place at the same level it grew before. Firm soil around the roots.

5 Water well right after planting; water frequently until plants become established and new growth has started. Once that happens, plants fill in quickly. The photo at *right* was taken six weeks after the one *above*.

ANNUALS IN CONTAINERS

If you don't have much yard space, consider filling containers to overflowing with annual flowers. Instant color from these flowers can have a dramatic impact on your deck or patio.

Container gardening has many advantages, including effectiveness and ease. Because there are no planting beds to prepare, you save time and energy. Even if ground space is at a premium in your yard, color can abound from containers set on patios, steps, paths, decks, and balconies. Containers can be put anywhere and moved about as your mood changes. If something doesn't look quite right, you can take it away, spruce it up, and bring it back.

TYPES OF CONTAINERS
■ In addition to traditional flowerpots, a wide variety of containers is available: barrels, tubs, boxes, baskets, urns, plastic pipe, tree stumps, and even bags of potting soil.

Almost any container will do, as long as it has good drainage. Several holes in the bottom are a must to keep roots from getting waterlogged. If you want to use a decorative container with a solid bottom, place your plants in a draining-type pot that can sit inside the decorative one. A layer of gravel in the bottom of the outer pot will help prevent overwatering.

PLANTING AND CARING
■ Use a soilless media of sphagnum peat moss (or other organic matter) with perlite or vermiculite in a 50/50 ratio. Adding sharp sand to the mix will help keep small containers from toppling over in windy spots.

Because you'll want instant effect, plant containers with purchased bedding plants or plants you started indoors, rather than with seed. Plant tightly for massed beauty.

Plants grown in containers need to be watered often because they dry out faster than they do in the ground. Every week or two while watering, add a soluble fertilizer at half or quarter strength to stimulate growth and constant flowering. To keep growth uniform, rotate the containers weekly if sunlight hits them unevenly. Pick faded blooms.

Plant pots with compact annuals that produce nonstop color, such as petunias, marigolds, pinks, sweet alyssum, impatiens, or geraniums (*left*). A tall plant, such as dracaena, will look good centered in a large pot, with ivy geraniums cascading over the rim. For best effect, keep everything in proportion.

HANGING BASKETS

There's something special about brightening up the sky overhead with flowering plants in baskets. Drab decks and patios come to life. Massive spaces can become defined. Harsh lines are softened. Windows and doors take on a new accent. Baskets, hanging from anything strong enough to support them, add a third dimension to the garden. Hanging containers come in various designs, sizes, shapes, and materials. For best results, you'll want to choose containers that are lightweight and have adequate drainage.

Watering is one of the most important requirements hanging baskets have. Because they are limited in size and often are in the wind, plants in baskets can dry out very rapidly; you may need to water every day.

The list of annual possibilities for your basket can be lengthy, and what you choose depends on your taste. You can plant a basket with one type of plant only, or mix and match a variety of plants. If you do the latter, be careful not to overdo with too many plant types or colors. Some good combinations are (1) begonias, alyssum, and pansies; (2) verbena and geraniums; (3) begonias and browallia; (4) marigolds, alyssum, and lobelia; and (5) petunias, geraniums, and lobelia.

Other excellent choices for solo or combination baskets include coleus, impatiens, lantana, nasturtium, portulaca, and black-eyed susan vine. A white or silver dusty-miller, or a long, trailing vine, will add grace and depth to your container planting.

1 To create a moss ball, fill a wire basket with moistened sphagnum peat moss until the wire is completely covered with the moss. Fill the center with a mixture of potting soil and peat or perlite.

2 Poke holes into the moss all the way around the sides, top, and bottom of the basket, and insert the plants. Because sphagnum peat moss dries out quickly, keep it moist at all times.

1 When planting a wooden basket, hold plants in place while adding the potting mix around the roots. Space plants evenly in the basket. Firm the soil and water well.

2 Secure wires with a pliers to make sure the basket will not fall. You can also use a chain or a rope, as long as it is durable enough not to break. Hang from a screw eye or cup hook.

STRAWBERRY JARS

Strawberry jars can be used to grow the bright-red fruits of their namesake, but more often, their pockets are packed with colorful annuals. Flowers that are especially suited for planting in strawberry jars are those that cascade, including petunia, lobelia, and impatiens.

For best effect, avoid using plants that will grow too large and hide the jar's interesting features. Keep the plants in the jar simple, using only a few plant types such as the New Guinea impatiens, sweet alyssum, zinnias, and wax begonias at *right*. Your strawberry jar can be instantly beautiful if you plant it with flowers in bloom or in bud. If you grow your annuals from seed, give them an early start indoors.

Whether you start from transplants or seeds, pick colors that complement the red in the clay. For a cooling color contrast, poke such white-flowering favorites as candytuft, sweet alyssum, or begonias into the pockets. Blue or violet will burst into life from ageratum, nierembergia, or lobelia. One of the most cheerful combinations can come from pansies; their "faces" will peek in all directions from the jar.

Your choices also will depend on where the jar will be placed. In a cool, moist, and shaded spot, try baby-blue-eyes, browallia, or mimulus. Out in the sun, marigolds, zinnias, and petunias will do best. In areas where it's very hot, drought-tolerant portulaca or vinca are good performers.

Plants in strawberry jars look their best when they are watered daily. Provide good drainage at the bottom so the lower plants don't become waterlogged while the top ones dry out. To keep plants blooming from spring till frost, remove flowers as soon as they fade. A light pruning in midsummer will keep growth neat and in check throughout the growing season.

Because large strawberry jars can be cumbersome, put them on casters to move them around easily on your patio or deck, or to rotate them so that sunlight hits them evenly. If plants start looking tired and bedraggled, simply move the jar out of sight while you spruce it up.

For a special effect, use different sizes of strawberry jars in a small cluster, or tie strawberry jars to your in-ground flower border by repeating the same varieties you used in the garden. If your jar will be on the porch or patio, choose a fragrant annual, such as sweet alyssum to add to your enjoyment.

1 Before planting a strawberry jar, make sure there's a thick layer of gravel in the bottom for drainage. Fill to within 1 inch of the top with moist potting soil and firm the soil.

2 Add plants by making a small hole in each pocket and tucking in 1 to 3 plants, depending on their mature size. Press roots down gently. Plant from the bottom up, turning the jar as you go.

3 Plant the top of the jar last, spacing plants evenly, yet tightly. After planting the jar, water thoroughly. Add diluted plant food to keep the plants in tip-top condition.

WINDOW BOXES

Windows offer more than a way to look in or out. They represent an integral part of the architecture of a home or building. Imagine the Swiss chalet, the cottage by the beach, or the colonial building without their unique windows and window boxes to complete the picture. No matter what style your house is, a window box can fit in, breaking up the monotony of a blank wall and tying the rest of the garden to your home.

A window box can be as simple as a shelf, mounted below a windowsill, that holds several pots, or as self-contained as a large rectangular box attached with brackets. If you make your own wooden window box, use a high quality grade of lumber and let it age naturally, or use a less expensive grade and paint it to match the window trim. The thicker the wood, the greater its insulating ability will be to keep the soil's temperature and moisture more constant. Make the box at least 8 inches wide and deep; its length will depend on the width of your window. It should have 1-inch drainage holes, and be hung with rustproof brackets.

Because you'll be enjoying your window boxes as much from the indoors as from the outdoors, choose filler plants with care. For best impact, use compact plants with flowers that bloom continuously and stay attractive for close viewing all summer long.

Place taller flowers, such as geraniums, salvia, marigolds, and zinnias, in the back. Petunias, ageratum, or nasturtium can fill out the center, and ivy geraniums, lobelia, or sweet alyssum can spill over the front rim. Spring bulbs also do well in window boxes; replace them with mums in the fall.

1 You can buy window boxes at a garden supply store, or make them yourself from redwood, cedar, or pressure-treated pine. The shape and size of your boxes will depend on your situation. Keep in mind that several small boxes will be easier to handle and position than a large one.

2 Before planting your window box, drill several holes in the bottom for good drainage. To prevent the holes from clogging, cover them with a small piece of window screening or a layer of gravel. Add potting soil until the box is two-thirds full.

3 After firming the soil gently with your hands, position the plants by gently pressing the roots into the soil. Then add potting soil to within 1 inch of the top of the box. The flowers should be spaced about 4 inches apart to allow room for growth.

4 After planting, move your window box to a protected area for a few days so the plants' roots can get established. If you put your window box in an exposed, windy spot right after planting, the flowers may be permanently damaged. The window box *above* contains Candidum caladiums and Little Pinkie vinca.

CARE AND MAINTENANCE

If a garden full of annual flowers is your goal, your care and maintenance program must begin with good soil preparation (see page 8) and well-organized planting (see page 98). After that, you and Mother Nature will work together to produce a garden spot covered with color and life.

FERTILIZING

■ Because annuals bloom for only one season, they can usually get by without being fed. Some annuals, including nasturtium, cleome, and portulaca, require no supplementary nourishment. Others, however, will perform better if they occasionally receive food in addition to their regular watering. For those that benefit from fertilizing, mix a balanced 5-10-5 food into the soil prior to planting. To keep annuals in top shape, feed them with a water-soluble fertilizer once a month to produce even growth and maximum flowering.

WATERING

■ Deep, infrequent watering will promote better root growth than frequent, light applications. Any of the methods outlined on page 10 will work fine for annuals. If you plan to cut flowers for indoor bouquets, avoid overhead watering, which can damage the blossoms. Where hot, dry weather prevails, choose a drought-resistant annual, such as portulaca, four-o'clock, celosia, cosmos, sunflower, or zinnia.

MULCHING

■ Mulch helps annuals grow by reducing weeds and conserving soil moisture. It also adds a clean, neat look to your flower bed. Apply a 3- to 4-inch layer of mulch around plants in the spring after your annuals are established. At the end of the season, spade organic mulches into the soil for a fertile planting bed the following year.

STAKING

■ Top-heavy or tall annuals will need to be staked to keep them from bending and breaking. Use a sturdy stake, tying it loosely to the plant with cord or a twist tie. Tying too tightly can pinch or damage the stem.

PRIMPING

■ Keep your garden neat by pulling weeds, removing faded flowers and discolored leaves, and pruning and trimming. Some annuals, such as petunias, may need to be cut back after their first flush of bloom to encourage a greater second bloom. This gardening chore will soon become a job of the past, however, because today's improved hybrids offer more bloom-power than their ancestors did.

After frost has blackened the tops of your annual garden in the fall, you can pull the plants or leave them to be incorporated into the soil next spring. Add to the compost pile any disease-free plants you pull.

PEST CONTROL

■ Most annuals are rarely bothered by insects or diseases. Zinnias, however, are susceptible to mildew. You can control this problem by planting zinnias in open areas with good air circulation, and by avoiding overhead watering systems that get the foliage wet.

Many annual flowers, such as the marigold *above,* should be removed as they fade. This simple procedure, called deadheading, ensures maximum and continuous blooming all summer. Clip or snap off dead flowers.

Petunias can get leggy. To keep them compact and to induce more blooming, pinch them back by removing stems at leaf joinings. You'll also encourage growth by regularly cutting flowers for indoor bouquets.

1 You can multiply some annuals, such as the coleus *above,* by taking cuttings and rooting them. For best results, clip a stem about 4 inches long with at least 4 leaves. Remove the lowest 2 leaves, and apply a rooting hormone to the bottom.

2 Insert the cutting into a growing media of premoistened sphagnum peat moss and/or sand. Place the pot in a plastic bag and set it in an area with good light, but not direct sun. In about 10 days, check for rooting by gently pulling on the cutting.

3 When cuttings have rooted, remove them from the rooting media and transplant them to containers or to the garden, depending on the time of year. Other annuals that can be grown from cuttings include impatiens, geraniums, and begonias.

Many annuals, such as sweet alyssum, lobelia, and petunia (*above*), may get too bushy and encroach on other flowers. Use hedge clippers or shears to keep them in check. They'll resume blooming soon after trimming.

Make your garden easy to maintain by selecting the proper plant for your climate. For example, pansies (*above*), nemesia, baby-blue-eyes, and salpiglossis love cool weather, making them poorly suited for hot, dry climates.

Drought-tolerant plants, such as the portulaca (*above*), vinca, dusty-miller, geranium, and gazania, thrive where summers are hot and dry. Plant these annuals in a sunny garden location that has well-drained soil.

110

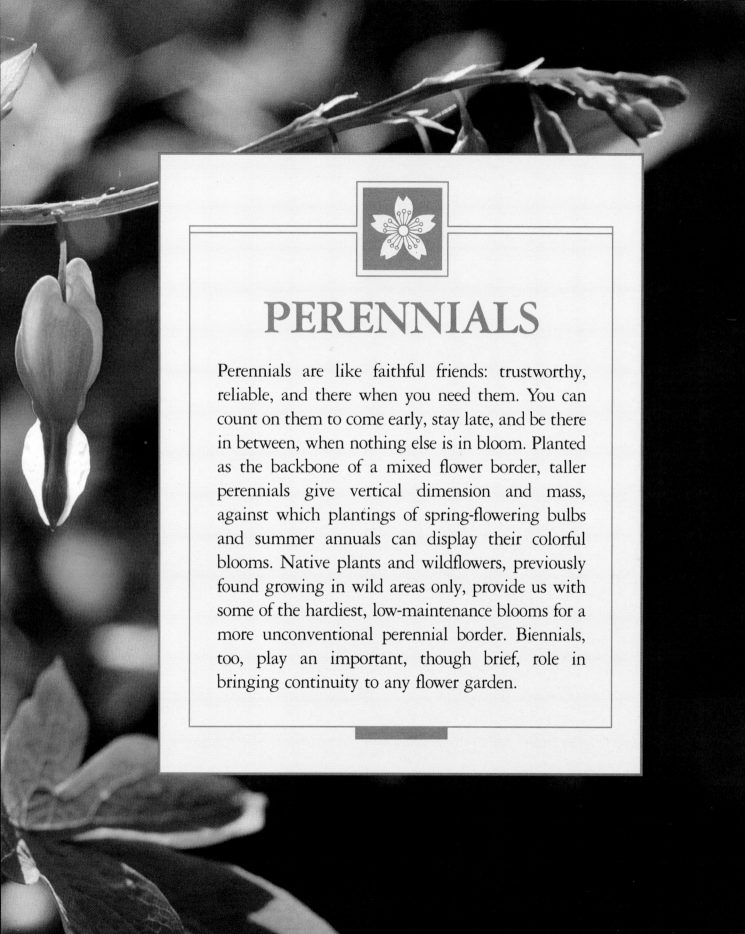

PERENNIALS

Perennials are like faithful friends: trustworthy, reliable, and there when you need them. You can count on them to come early, stay late, and be there in between, when nothing else is in bloom. Planted as the backbone of a mixed flower border, taller perennials give vertical dimension and mass, against which plantings of spring-flowering bulbs and summer annuals can display their colorful blooms. Native plants and wildflowers, previously found growing in wild areas only, provide us with some of the hardiest, low-maintenance blooms for a more unconventional perennial border. Biennials, too, play an important, though brief, role in bringing continuity to any flower garden.

PERENNIALS IN THE LANDSCAPE

Large or small, formal or informal, high- or low-maintenance, no garden is complete without a selection of perennials to lead it through the gardening season. Year after year, perennials offer an everchanging framework of color, filling borders with lovely flowers and a variety of foliage textures and shades of green. Unlike annuals, perennials don't require the time and expense of yearly replanting. Most will grow and bloom for many years without a lot of pampering. This sense of permanence adds continuity to the garden.

Whatever your soil and climatic conditions, you can find perennials in a wide selection of sizes, shapes, and colors to fulfill them. Perennials such as (front to back) Gold Drop rudbeckia, phlox, bee balm, bellflower, cimicifuga, and ligularia pack the sunny border *below* with color in late summer.

Use perennials to take advantage of nooks and crannies you may have previously overlooked. A little ingenuity turned the thin strips of soil on either side of the front walk at *right* into a festival of flowers. Columbine, daylily, and iris mix with annuals like geranium, petunia, portulaca, zinnia, alyssum, and dwarf marigold to fill both beds to overflowing. Early in the spring, a variety of bulbs can fill the same beds for many months of color.

PERENNIALS IN THE LANDSCAPE

Careful planning will reward you with a mixed perennial border that is abloom from spring to frost. Because most plants blossom for just a few weeks, you must plant a variety of perennials that bloom at successive intervals. To have constant bloom, assign each perennial to a spot where it will provide color at a specific period during the season.

Make your border at least 4 to 6 feet deep, and plant perennials so they're tapered in height. If the border is backed by a wall or fence, plant tall varieties in back and low growers in front. To enjoy an island bed from all sides, plant taller perennials in the center of the bed and have shorter plants radiate out to the edges. Group three or more of one variety and color in drifts for best visual impact.

In early summer, the garden *below* comes alive with spikes of foxglove in back, masses of peonies, columbine, and iris in the middle, and dianthus in front. Throughout the summer, other perennials will take over, such as phlox, lythrum, liatris, shasta daisy, and aster.

Combine perennials that bloom at different times to ensure a succession of color throughout the season. To make planning easier, the mixed flower garden at *right* is divided into smaller, easy-to-manage sections. In spring, bloom comes from columbine, forget-me-not, bleeding-heart, peony, iris, coralbell, and Virginia bluebell. Joining these perennials in summer are gaillardia, baptisia, hollyhock, delphinium, phlox, Shasta daisy, astilbe, daylily, lupine, pinks, yarrow, and hardy lily. Late summer brings a grand finale of hardy asters and chrysanthemums.

Choose a color scheme for your border, too. For bright splashy colors, use a lot of reds, bright yellows, blues, and purples. A softer look can be made with pinks, blues, pale yellows, and white.

Many perennials will perform brightly without sunshine. In the shady border at *right,* sedum, astilbe, Siberian iris, rudbeckia, *Lobelia splendens,* and *Sanguisorba canadensis* grow in front of the tall Rocket ligularia. Other perennials that are made for the shade are bleeding-heart, hosta, fern, and columbine.

Nature's woodlands also provide us with a large family of flowers that bloom without the sun. Some favorite shade-loving wildflowers are bloodroot, dog-tooth violet, dutchman's-breeches, wild geranium, mayapple, jacob's-ladder, wild ginger, hepatica, jack-in-the-pulpit, sweet william, spring beauty, solomon's-seal, and trillium. To leave natural areas undisturbed, buy wildflower transplants or seeds from a local or mail-order nursery.

PLANNING A PERENNIAL BORDER

There's more to perennial gardening than filling a border with pretty flowers. A prizewinning perennial border is one that gets its natural look from careful planning on the part of the gardener. When perennials are combined attractively in an informal design, each one gets a turn to be the spotlighted star of an ongoing floral show.

COLOR
■ Color can be the framework of your garden design, providing accent, balance, repetition, and excitement. When combining perennials, choose a color scheme for each season, using one main color as a backbone: for example, yellow for spring, pink for early summer, blue for midsummer, and gold for fall. Blues and violets are cooler colors, and

will make the garden appear larger; bolder reds, oranges, and yellows will add warmth to the design.

Select a few plants in each chosen color range, then sprinkle in a few secondary perennials in complementary colors. To avoid a checkerboard effect with small isolated spots of color, plant each perennial en masse and repeat throughout the border. For contrast, put similar or opposite colors near the massed colors. With orange daylilies, for example, use yellow coreopsis or clear blue anchusa.

SHAPE AND TEXTURE
■ Variety in form and foliage adds spice to a garden. Use a mixture of mat and cushion plants, medium- and large-size mounded plants, and plants with spiked

blossoms. Foliage types that you can choose from include coarse or soft, lance-shaped or rounded, and flat or glossy. Base your final selections on a variety of plant heights, so that plants of all sizes appear in the garden design.

STYLE
■ Formal or informal? This will be determined by your taste and the style of your home. Formal gardens are symmetrical; the more popular informal gardens are amorphous and most effective when laid out in curved drifts.

If you're new at perennial garden design, visit other gardens and note what blooms at various times, which plants create appealing combinations and contrasts, and which textures and colors can be integrated into your design.

EARLY SUMMER
■ The ultimate challenge to any perennial gardener is to design a border with color and interest all summer. Any planning you do before planting will help eliminate the need to make changes later. The garden at *right* begins the summer with blooms from lythrum, daylily, black-eyed susan, gaillardia, and lily. Other perennials that bloom in early summer are gas plant, shasta daisy, thermopsis, and Canterbury-bells. All-season color in front comes from annuals, such as petunia, marigold, ageratum, zinnia, and salvia.

Before selecting plants, make note of the amount of sun the border will receive. The plants listed above are sun worshipers. Choose others if your garden will be shaded.

MIDSUMMER

■ In midsummer, clumps of white and pink phlox, blue and purple delphinium, liatris, and veronica join the parade of perennial color. Other excellent profuse bloomers include balloon flower, scabiosa, lavender, cupid's-dart, butterfly weed, marguerite, snakeroot, globe thistle, hosta, coralbells, and bee-balm. Black-eyed susan, coreopsis, and blanketflower continue to flower from earlier in the summer.

Check the hardiness of the plants you have selected for your border and make sure they will survive the rigors of your winters. Draw the plan out to scale on graph paper to know how many plants to buy and how close together to plant them. Determine spacing between the plants by their size at maturity.

LATE SUMMER

■ Late summer announces the arrival of chrysanthemums. Other perennials that offer autumn bloom include sedum, aster, goldenrod, helianthus, hardy ageratum, turtlehead, and physostegia.

Soil is an important element to consider when designing your perennial garden. Although you can and should improve garden soil before planting, some soil conditions will limit your planting choices. An always-moist soil, for example, won't provide a healthy home for perennials that require a well-drained soil. Fortunately, a number of perennials, including bergenia, filipendula, the cardinal flower, lysimachia, lythrum, forget-me-not, globe flower, and Japanese and Siberian iris prefer to have their feet wet.

GALLERY OF PERENNIALS

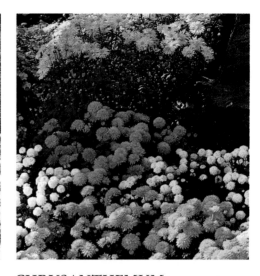

ASTILBE hybrids
Astilbe x arendsi

Astilbe are attractive perennials for the shady garden border. Flowers produced in early to midsummer are feathery, pyramidal spikes in pink, white, red, or salmon. The foliage, with its finely cut, roselike leaves, is attractive even when the plant is not in bloom.
SOIL: Prefers moist soil, but does well in dry spots also.
LIGHT: Partial sun to heavy shade. For best growth, give higher light.
HARDINESS: Zone 6
COMMENTS: There are many good hybrid varieties. Fanal, Peach Blossom, Deutschland, Rheinland, and Superba are the best known.

Start plants in early spring from seed or by division. For best growth, keep plants well watered and fed. A two- to three-inch layer of mulch around the plant will keep roots cool and moist.

CANDYTUFT
Iberis sempervirens

Candytuft is an excellent choice for the rock garden, borders, or edgings, because it grows only 8 to 12 inches tall. It produces tiny, white flowers in flat umbels or clusters in mid- to late spring. Foliage is evergreen, with long, narrow, shiny leaves that lay in a whorl around the stem.
SOIL: Rich, well drained
LIGHT: Full sun
HARDINESS: Zone 3
COMMENTS: The most popular varieties include: Little Gem, Snowflake, Purity, Autumn Snow, and Pygmy. The variety Autumn Snow is unique, because it blooms in both spring and fall.

After candytuft blooms, cut it back with a hedge cutter. This will keep it compact and ensure maximum flowering the following year. Candytuft grows easily from cuttings or seeds.

CHRYSANTHEMUM
Chrysanthemum species and hybrids

Chrysanthemums are the crowning glory of the fall garden with all sizes of flowers in every color but true blue. Flower shapes include single, semidouble, anemone, pompon, incurve, reflexed, spoon, quill, or spider. The height of mums varies from low-growing cushion types to football mums several feet tall.
SOIL: Rich, well drained, heavily fed, and well watered
LIGHT: Full sun
HARDINESS: Zone 5
COMMENTS: To produce full flower heads, pinch mums from early spring to mid-July. There are hundreds of varieties that are excellent in the garden or in containers. Start new plants from seeds, root divisions, and stem cuttings. Or buy started plants in midsummer.

Shasta and painted daisies are relatives of the chrysanthemum. They start blooming earlier in the season.

COREOPSIS (tickseed)
Coreopsis species

One of the most dependable and long-est-blooming perennials is the coreopsis. Flowers, which appear from June until frost, are yellow, daisylike, and either single or double. The plant itself grows 24 to 30 inches tall and is relatively care free. Some leaves are large and solid; some of them are lobed. The threadleaf coreopsis (*C. verticillata*) has very fine foliage.

SOIL: Any type
LIGHT: Full sun
HARDINESS: Zone 6
COMMENTS: To keep coreopsis at its peak of bloom, keep cutting away the flowers after they fade. If you enjoy cut flowers for the house, coreopsis is an excellent choice for your cutting garden. To propagate coreopsis, grow them from seed or divisions, lifted and replanted in either fall or spring.

DAYLILY
Hemerocallis species and varieties

From the Greek word, meaning "beautiful for a day," the hemerocallis or daylily is one of the best plants for the perennial border or for planting along roadsides or on slopes. Their tight root systems make them good for erosion control. Lilylike flowers bloom in every color except true blue and pure white, on plants that can range from 18 to 36 inches tall. Swordlike leaves are relatively free from problems.

SOIL: Any type soil. Water needed only during droughts.
LIGHT: Full sun or part shade
HARDINESS: Zone 5
COMMENTS: Daylilies are grown for their lovely flowers, which have been greatly improved by breeding. Tens of thousands of varieties are now available. Although each flower lasts for only a day, the plants will be in flower for weeks. By combining varieties, you'll have color for months.

DELPHINIUM
Delphinium species and hybrids

Dramatic is the best word to describe delphiniums. Although there are some dwarf varieties available, most reach 4 to 6 feet tall. Borne on long spikes, blooms appear in early summer and again in fall. True blue and purple are the most-recognized colors.

SOIL: Deep, rich, and light, with a pH of neutral or slightly alkaline. Soil should also be well drained, to prevent crown rot, and very fertile. Water well at all times.
LIGHT: Full sun
HARDINESS: Zone 3
COMMENTS: Delphiniums prefer a cool, moist climate, so they are difficult to grow in hot and dry areas. They are short-lived plants, and will need to be replaced every few years. Because they grow tall, they must be staked. When choosing varieties, look at the Pacific Giant and Connecticut Yankee hybrids for good performance.

GALLERY OF PERENNIALS

HOSTA (plantain lily, funkia)
Hosta species

Although the hosta does flower, it is primarily known as a foliage plant for beds, borders, or as a ground cover. Leaves range from lance-shape to round, in all sizes. Leaf colors, patterns and textures include blue, green, variegated, smooth, and quilted. A flower spike appears in summer, with lilylike blooms of white, blue, or pale lavender. **SOIL:** Not fussy about soil, but will do better if soil is rich.
LIGHT: Part shade
HARDINESS: Zone 3
COMMENTS: Hosta is one of the longest-lived perennials and one of the most care-free. It is rarely bothered by pests and will tolerate a variety of adverse growing conditions. To increase plants, dig and divide. Roots are tough; don't be afraid to pull them apart. Good choices include: *H. ventricosa, H. sieboldiana, H. undulata, H. plantaginea, H. decorata,* and *H. fortunei albomarginata.*

IRIS
Iris species and hybrids

Of all the many types of iris grown, bearded iris is the most common. Plant height varies from only a few inches in the bulbous iris to the more common varieties growing 3 to 4 feet high. Flowers are solids or bicolors, in any color imaginable. Foliage is swordlike. If leaf ends dry out, cut them off with sharp shears for neatness.
SOIL: Average, well-drained, sandy soil, with a dry, alkaline consistency
LIGHT: Full sun
HARDINESS: Zone 4
COMMENTS: Bearded irises have many relatives that do well in the garden. Short, crested types, such as *I. cristata,* take a little more shade. The beardless iris likes a moister soil. Among the beardless are Japanese, Siberian, and water iris. Bulbous irises include Dutch iris and *I. reticulata.* Use them to line a border or mass them in a rock garden.

PEONY
Paeonia hybrids

Garden dependability is synonymous with the peony. Long-lived plants form 2- to 4-foot-tall clumps and shrublike bunches. Flowers come in every shade except blue, but most are in tones of pink and red. Flower shapes are single; Japanese (single with large yellow centers); anemone (like the Japanese, with a powder-puff center); and double. A peony does best where winter temperatures drop to near or below zero.
SOIL: Slightly acidic; must have excellent drainage
LIGHT: Full sun
HARDINESS: Zone 5
COMMENTS: There are literally more peonies than you could ever grow. In choosing, look for your favorite color combinations. The blooms are all fragrant and fill the garden or home with a delicious scent. Since blooms do get heavy, they will usually need to be staked. Ants love peony buds, but generally do no harm.

PHLOX
Phlox species

The phlox of the summer garden is a tall—to 6 feet—stately plant with clusters of flat, 5-petaled flowers appearing in mid- to late summer. Flower colors are in the white, red, pink, blue, and violet shades. Many have a contrasting eye. In contrast to this tall plant (*P. paniculata*), lower-growing phlox (*P. subulata* and *P. divaricata*) reach only 6 to 18 inches and are lovely in a rock garden. The former has pink or white flowers in the spring; the latter has blue flowers at the same time.
SOIL: Well-drained soil, kept cool with a mulch
LIGHT: Full sun
HARDINESS: Zone 5
COMMENTS: Phlox, an old-fashioned favorite, is subject to mildew. To prevent this, leave room between plants for air to circulate. Phlox should be grown from cuttings or divisions, because they revert to their original purple color when grown from seed.

POPPY, ORIENTAL
Papaver orientale

The Oriental poppy is one of the top perennials that should be in every garden. Blooming in late spring or early summer, poppies have large, papery flowers of white, red, orange, or pink around a black center. The flowers can be single or double, and can be up to 6 inches across. Foliage is coarse and hairy; stems grow 2 to 4 feet high.
SOIL: Average, well drained. Plants will rot in a too-wet soil.
LIGHT: Full sun
HARDINESS: Zone 4
COMMENTS: Poppy foliage disappears after the plants bloom and reappears in early fall. Therefore, be prepared to surround the area with annuals so the flower bed will not be bare all summer. Poppies like cold winters and make excellent cut flowers.

YARROW
Achillea species

Yarrow is a vigorous perennial used mostly in mixed beds, but sometimes useful in rock gardens or borders as well. Some varieties are as low-growing as 6 inches, but most reach 24 to 36 inches in height. Good for dried bouquets, flowers are golden yellow or reddish violet. Another species, known as sneezewort, has white flowers. Blooms are flat clusters of tiny flowers; the foliage is attractive and fernlike.
SOIL: Any soil—even the poorest—is acceptable. Yarrow is happy with dry soil. It even thrives in droughts.
LIGHT: Full sun
HARDINESS: Zone 3
COMMENTS: Yarrow can become weedy and overgrown, so give it an annual checkup and remove any unwanted plantlets. Flowers appear in June and again in September if cut back. Staking may be necessary. For beds or drying, try Coronation Gold, Moonshine, and Fire King.

DIVIDING AND PLANTING IRISES AND PEONIES

You can weave an exotic tapestry of flowers into your landscape plan with irises. Exceptionally hardy, irises adapt to most garden sites and come in a wide variety of colors and sizes. They thrive in little space with minimal care.

The bearded iris is the most common member of the iris family. Bearded types are divided into tall, intermediate, and dwarf varieties. Members of the intermediate group (*above*) are a little shorter and bloom a bit earlier than tall bearded irises. Other iris types include bulbous, spuria, Japanese, Siberian, and Dutch.

To keep established clumps of iris in top form, dig and divide the plants whenever they grow too crowded (usually every three to five years). The Siberian iris rarely needs dividing. Late summer and early fall are the best times to plant or divide all three types of bearded iris. These plants grow from long, fleshy surface roots called rhizomes. Use the following instructions when you plant a new iris or divide an older clump into smaller plants.

1 Use a sharp knife to separate an iris clump; each division should have at least one growing point (or fan of leaves) and a few inches of healthy rhizome with feeder roots.

2 Before you replant divisions, trim foliage to a fan shape, cutting it back to a height of 5 inches. Cut out borers (pinkish-white grubs) you find in rhizomes.

3 Dig a hole large enough to hold the division's root system. Form a mound of dirt in the center of the hole; spread the roots evenly over the mound.

4 Add soil until the rhizome is 1 inch below the surface. Water thoroughly. To eliminate weed competition, mulch with compost or shredded bark.

Peonies can grow undisturbed in the same spot for a decade or two, but to increase the number of plants, dig up clumps and divide every 5 to 10 years. Fall is the best time to plant or divide and transplant peonies.

Most cultivated varieties of peonies are hybrids of the herbaceous Chinese peony (*Paeonia lactiflora*). Producing spectacular, 10-inch-diameter blooms, Chinese peonies are available in single, semidouble, double, anemone (*above*), and Japanese forms. Herbaceous types grow 18 to 30 inches tall.

Showy tree peonies (*P. suffruticosa*) bloom earlier than Chinese types and bear as many as 80 giant, crinkled blossoms on one plant. Unlike their more tender herbaceous relatives, these 4- to 7-foot-tall, woody shrubs do not die back during the winter.

A clump of peonies will bloom every spring for many years, even decades, with minimal care. To extend their flowering season from early spring to early summer, plant a mix of early-, mid-, and late-season varieties.

1 To divide peonies, dig a shallow trench around the edge of the clump. Pry under the root mass with a spade and lift from the soil. Cut off tops of plants.

2 Wash all soil from the roots so you can see where the eyes (buds) are. Divide the clump with a sharp knife; each division should have at least three eyes.

3 To plant, dig a hole 2 feet deep in a sunny spot. Fill the hole with enriched soil until the eyes of the division are 1½ to 2 inches below ground level. Spread the roots out evenly.

4 Fill in the hole with soil, being careful not to break off any of the eyes. Water well and mulch if you live in a cold climate. Peonies look best in clumps with each division spaced 3 feet apart.

125

DIVIDING AND PLANTING DAYLILIES AND POPPIES

"Beautiful for a day" is the Greek meaning of *Hemerocallis,* the genus name for daylily. Though individual blooms last just a day, other flower buds on the same stalk (most plants have about 20 buds) keep the color show going.

Offered in an array of colors and bi-colors, daylily blossoms vary in size from 3 to 11 inches across and come in either single or double forms. Many varieties have lovely ruffled edges. Plant height ranges from the 15-inch miniatures to the 3-foot standards. For color all summer, select varieties from early-, mid-, and late-blooming types.

Daylilies will flourish almost anywhere. They bloom more abundantly in the sun, but they also can tolerate some shade. Although daylilies can be divided and transplanted any time the ground is soft enough to dig, spring and fall are the best times. Divide when the plants look overcrowded (every 4 or 5 years). Because plants moved in spring may not bloom until the following year, you may want to wait until fall to divide your daylilies.

1 To divide daylilies, dig a clump with a sharp spade. Daylily roots are resilient, so don't be afraid to use force to loosen the clump from the ground.

2 If you transplant in the fall, trim off the top of the foliage before you replant the divisions. For spring transplants, leave the foliage intact and allow it to grow.

3 Cut clumps apart with a sharp knife. Dig a hole from 10 to 15 inches deep, depending on the size of the root system. Make a mound of soil in the center of the hole.

4 Set daylily divisions at the same depth the plant grew before, and spread roots evenly over the soil mound. Tamp down soil and water thoroughly.

Blooming like tufts of tissue paper in early summer, Oriental poppies perform yearly encores with a minimum of care. Poppies come in both single- and double-bloom forms, in colors ranging from white to shades of orange and red.

Late summer, when the plants are dormant, is the best time to plant new poppies. Start these plants from nursery-grown roots, and space them 18 to 24 inches apart. Because the foliage on Oriental poppy dies back and disappears in midsummer after plants are finished blooming, plant poppies with annuals and other perennials that will camouflage the ripening leaves and fill the gaps left in the border.

Poppies will grow indefinitely without getting overcrowded, but you can divide them to increase your supply of plants. The best time to divide existing clumps is in early fall, when plants send up fresh leaves in preparation for the following year's bloom. That way, you can use the outline of foliage as a guide for digging. Avoid breaking the long, brittle roots when you dig.

1 Plant dormant nursery-grown roots of Oriental poppies in late summer. Established clumps are best divided in early fall, as soon as fresh foliage appears.

2 Dig a hole slightly larger than the root system for each plant and set the root so its scaly crown can be placed 2 to 3 inches below the soil surface.

3 To improve soil drainage, work in plenty of well-rotted compost or manure. Fill the hole with soil, and water well to eliminate air pockets around the plant's roots.

4 After watering, firm the soil around the plant with your hands. In cold climates, poppies will need winter protection. Cover the plants with leaves or straw.

CARE AND MAINTENANCE

Perennials can be grown from seed, nursery-grown roots, or divisions of established plants. Although each perennial has its own care requirements, follow these general tips to ensure success in the border.

SOIL PREPARATION
■ Because a perennial grows in the same spot for many years, preparing soil in the bed is the first important step toward getting a plant of top-notch quality. As early in the spring as the ground can be worked, turn the soil the full depth of the spade. Mix in a generous amount of organic matter and a fertilizer rich in phosphorus, such as bonemeal or superphosphate. Rake the ground level.

HOW TO PLANT
■ Dig holes big enough to handle the large roots of many perennials. Set plants at the same level they grew before and tamp them carefully into place without breaking the roots. After planting, mark the location of the new plants and water well. Space plants according to the distances recommended in the chart on page 120; spacing should accommodate their size at maturity and allow good air circulation. Watering is particularly important with new plants until they become well established.

POST-PLANTING CARE
■ In early spring, apply an all-purpose fertilizer, such as 5-10-5, and water in lightly. For an extra boost during the blooming season, apply water-soluble plant food to the foliage and soil.

After the soil has warmed up, apply a summer mulch to keep the soil cool and moist and to keep weeds down.

Tall, top-heavy perennials, such as hollyhock, delphinium (*above*), and foxglove, often fall over and need help to stay upright. In early spring, set stakes in the soil and tie the stems as they grow.

To keep perennials blooming, remove flowers as soon as they fade. Known as deadheading, this procedure forces fresh growth and encourages new bud formation.

Other perennials, such as black-eyed susan (*above*) and baby's-breath, have bushy plants on wiry stems that arch over. Set several stakes around the clump and hold together with twine.

WINTER PROTECTION

■ After the first killing frost in the fall, cut and remove all dead stalks and trim stems to within an inch or two of the ground. Next, apply a winter mulch of leaves or straw. If rainfall has been light during summer and fall months, deeply water your perennials.

Oriental poppies and Madonna lilies send up growth in the fall that need extra care. A pot placed over the foliage will provide good protection, or build a tent over the plant with two wire hoops covered with heavy cloth or paper.

DIVIDING

■ Perennials will bloom more vigorously if they're divided every few years. A plant needs dividing when it shows weak or dying center growth, crowds out neighboring plants, or produces less-than-spectacular blooms.

Most plants should be divided in early spring, as soon as new growth appears. Others—including iris, lily, and Oriental poppy—do better if you divide them in late summer or fall. Follow the same steps for transplanting as you would for setting in new plants.

As soon as frost has blackened the tops of perennials, cut and remove dead stalks, leaving just an inch or two so you can tell in the spring where the plants are.

Any garden can use a well-designed cold frame. The cold frame *above* has a slanted top and a back several inches higher than the front. The removable top is made of inexpensive plastic.

Use cold frames for hardening off new seedlings in spring, and overwintering (providing a warmer winter home for plants) summer seedlings and tender perennials dug before fall frost.

After you remove dead foliage and other debris, cover beds with a winter mulch of evergreen boughs, leaves, or straw in cold climates. Hold mulch in place by anchoring chicken wire over it.

WILDFLOWERS

Tough landscaping problems in your yard will knuckle under to native plants and wildflowers. These sturdy, low-maintenance plants are debuting in gardens after growing wild in woodlands, prairies, and deserts, and along roadsides. Native plants and wildflowers naturally solve such challenges as steep slopes, densely shaded areas, low-lying wet spots, and dry hot places.

Study the natural conditions in your yard, including soil fertility, drainage, and the amount of sunlight or shade. Then match this information with the plants that are suited for your situation. Plants that are indigenous to your area will probably work best for you. Rather than remove plants from the wild, purchase seeds or plants from nurseries or mail-order catalogs.

The small woodland garden at *right* performs much like a natural forest. Such early-blooming wildflowers as jack-in-the-pulpit, marsh marigold, trillium, and bloodroot are followed by an equally brilliant summer show of royal fern, bluet, mayapple, bleeding-heart, Virginia bluebell, and wild geranium. True to nature's woodlands, these native gems are happier when left completely undisturbed.

Meadow flowers can be the ticket you need if you have a large sunny area in your yard that you'd rather not mow. Many seed companies are now offering native seed mixes, packaged for specific regions. Although plants spread quickly, brighter rewards will show up the second year. Each year, a different combination of plants will bloom.

WILDFLOWERS FOR SUN

- Aster, wild
- Black-eyed susan
- Blanketflower
- Blue gentian
- Blue lobelia
- Butterfly weed
- California poppy
- Evening primrose
- Forget-me-not
- Liatris
- Marsh marigold
- Purple coneflower
- Queen-Anne's-lace
- Rose mallow
- Sunflower
- Tickseed
- Virginia bluebells
- Yarrow

WILDFLOWERS FOR SHADE

- Bloodroot
- Cardinal flower
- Columbine
- Crested iris
- Dog-tooth violet
- Dutchman's-breeches
- Ferns
- Foamflower
- Jack-in-the-pulpit
- Jacob's-ladder
- Mayapple
- Partridgeberry
- Shooting-star
- Solomon's-seal
- Spiderwort
- Trillium
- Violet
- Wild ginger

DUTC
Dicentra

This clo
has fine
on the
white,
old-fash
down t
plant is
with fl
foliage
SOIL:
LIGHT
HARD
COMM
and dis
pared
necessa
the wo
areas.
like to
increas
root di

Think ahead to next su
planting biennials this
to grow, biennials hav
cycle. They produce
year and blossoms and s
year, then die. Dependi
climate and plant hard.
some biennials behave n
nials. Foxglove, sweet w
lyhock, for example, wil
themselves after bloomii
volunteers the next year

FAVORITE BIENNIA
■ The viola (*Viola tricolor*
choice for edging. Availa
grown plants, violas often
annuals. Either discard vi
bloom, or allow them t

GALLERY OF BIENNIALS

CANTERBURY-BELLS
Campanula medium

Try canterbury-bells for middle-of-the-border color. These showy biennials grow 24 to 36 inches tall, with long spikes of white, pink, yellow, lavender, or blue flowers. The 2- to 3-inch-long blooms are cup- or bell-shaped. Both single- and double-flower types are available, blooming in early summer.
SOIL: Rich, well drained, well watered
LIGHT: Full sun or light shade
HARDINESS: Zone 4
COMMENTS: Several closely related plants also are assets to the flower garden. *C. calycanthema*—commonly called cup and saucer—is named for the flower shape which resembles a cup sitting on a saucer. The carpathian bellflower (*C. carpatica*) is a tufted perennial, 1 foot tall. *C. elatines* has matlike growth and peach-leaved bellflower (*C. persicifolia*) grows in erect clumps.

ENGLISH DAISY
Bellis perennis

A low-growing (4 to 6 inches tall) plant, the English daisy has asterlike flowers of white, pink, red, or purple that bloom all spring. Flowers have big yellow centers and somewhat paperlike petals. Single, semidouble, and double varieties are all available. Blooms appear above a rosette of basal leaves.
SOIL: Light, rich, moist; keep well fertilized and well watered.
LIGHT: Full sun, light shade in hot and dry areas
HARDINESS: Zone 3
COMMENTS: English daisy, as you might guess, does best in cool and damp climates. Its use extends to rock gardens and borders. In the south, English daisy is a good winter-bloomer. However, it can become weedy and encroach into the lawn. For continuous bloom, start new plants yearly.

FOXGLOVE
Digitalis purpurea

When you need a tall, spiked plant for the back of the border, think of foxglove. Stems contain spikes of graceful, drooping, tube-shaped, 1-inch flowers that bloom in the early summer. Flower colors include red, pink, lavender, yellow, cream, and white with spots on the inside of the blooms.
SOIL: Rich, loose soil with excellent drainage, kept moist
LIGHT: Part shade
HARDINESS: Zone 5
COMMENTS: These tall, stately 4- to 6-foot plants deserve a spot in any garden. Since they are so tall, it may be necessary to stake the plants to keep them upright, especially in the wind. Digitalis leaves are the source of the heart medication with the same name. These leaves should not be eaten by humans or animals.

Lunaria annua
Money plant, honesty

An old-fashioned garden plant, known as the money plant because its seedpods look like silver dollars. Lunaria is an easy-to-grow, 3-foot-tall biennial. Fragrant white, purple, or pink flowers growing in clusters appear in early summer. During the second year, the round, flat, translucent pods appear, which can be used in dried bouquets. Coarse foliage covers stems.

SOIL: Any type
LIGHT: Part shade
HARDINESS: Zone 4
COMMENTS: If you enjoy arranging dried flowers, this plant is a must for your garden and winter bouquets. When the fruits—or seedpods—are mature, cut them, rub the coverings off with your fingers, and hang them in a cool, airy place to dry. Lunaria self-sows very easily, so you will need to take some time to remove unwanted seedlings each year.

PANSY
Viola tricolor hortensis

The popular pansy blooms in early spring and into summer where climatic conditions are right. The happy "faces" of the flowers are their primary appeal in solids or bicolors of red, purple, bronze, yellow, blue, white, pink, lavender, or orange. Blooms measure up to 4 inches across on 7- to 9-inch plants.

SOIL: Rich, moist soil
LIGHT: Full- to half-day sun in cool areas; partial shade in warm climates
HARDINESS: Zone 6
COMMENTS: Although pansies are biennials, they can also be treated as annuals. In marginally cold areas, mulch them lightly with leaves if you want to winter them over. They should also be mulched in summer to keep the soil cool. For maximum bloom, pick faded flowers. When shopping for pansies, look for Universal, Crystal Bowl, Majestic Giants, or Imperial hybrids. Newer strains are more heat resistant.

SWEET WILLIAM
Dianthus barbatus

Useful as a plant for edging, mixed borders, or the rock garden, the sweet william belongs to the family of the garden pinks. They don't get the name from their color—they're not all pink—but from their petal edges, which look like they were cut with a pinking shears. Flat flowers in round clusters are pink, white, red, or purple, with some double varieties. Blooms appear in early summer. Foliage looks like grass. Plants can reach 6 to 24 inches tall.

SOIL: Sandy, well drained, alkaline; kept moist and cool
LIGHT: Full sun
HARDINESS: Zone 4
COMMENTS: Plants prefer a cool and moist climate. Keep well mulched to keep soil cool, and protect during the winter in borderline areas. Sweet william can be treated as an annual with started plants in spring. It sometimes acts as a perennial by self-sowing.

BULBS

The old saying about good things coming in small packages couldn't be truer than with bulbs. Inside layers of scales or under a nondescript, brown skin lies one of Mother Nature's most inventive creations. A bulb is more than a root with potential to grow—it's a self-contained unit of roots, stems, and flowers, plus a food storage system triggered into motion by time and temperature. Closely related to bulbs (and discussed in this chapter because of similar growth requirements) are corms, tubers, tuberous roots, and rhizomes. They, too, store food, grow, bloom, restock on food, and go dormant until the following spring, summer, or fall, when it's time for nature to repeat its cycle.

BULBS IN THE LANDSCAPE

Nothing says "spring" better than a magnificent display of blooms that have grown from bulbs, especially when that display is tastefully integrated into your home's landscape. Long before any color bursts from other plants, shoots from such early-blooming bulbs as winter aconite (eranthis) and snowdrop (galanthus) poke their heads through the thawing soil. Many will blossom even when snow clings to the ground.

A little later, while days are still bleak and trees and shrubs still bare, crocus, Grecian windflower (anemone), Siberian squill (scilla), glory-of-the-snow (chionodoxa), and puschkinia begin to show off their blossoms. Because these bulbs bloom before grass starts to grow, they can be naturalized in the lawn, like the crocus, anemone, and scilla *below*.

Late spring heralds a mixed chorus of blooms from such bulbs as tulip, hyacinth, daffodil, snowflake (leucojum), fritillaria, oxalis, and allium. Planted en masse, these larger bulbs—such as the tulips and hyacinths at *right*—help fill the color void between spring's flowering trees and shrubs and summer's annuals and perennials.

Plant bulbs where you and passersby can most enjoy them. Along with growing in the lawn, these spring charmers do well around a base of trees near the house, or in small clumps at the front door. Squeeze them into the corner of a rock garden or use them as a border in front of a foundation planting. For continuous and everchanging color, select different types of flowers with complementary heights and colors.

HARDY LILIES

Hardy lilies were the backbone of many gardens in our grandmothers' day. These dependable old-time favorites also are worthy of a star position in modern-day perennial borders. Reaching 6 inches across, lily flowers cluster atop a straight stem 2 to 6 feet tall, with anywhere from three to 15 blooming at one time. Blossoms come in solid, spotted, or striped forms, in shades of red, orange, yellow, white, pink, and lavender. Some have a heavy fragrance.

HOW TO PLANT LILIES

■ Lilies like a spot in the sun or very light shade. Mix plenty of organic matter into the soil before planting to give roots good drainage. For best performance, plant most lilies 4 to 8 inches deep (Madonna lilies and Martagon lilies should be planted 1 to 2 inches deep). Add bonemeal to the bottom of each planting hole. Keep the soil moist, but not soggy, at all times. Mulch will help keep roots cool.

Fall is the best time to plant lilies. Because lily bulbs are never completely dormant, plant them immediately. If you have to delay planting, don't let the bulbs dry out. Planting should be completed by the first frost. For winter protection, cover plants with a generous layer of straw.

When lilies start to grow in spring, apply a balanced fertilizer. Feed them monthly after that until plants finish blooming. Some taller lilies may need to be staked. Use a bamboo stick that will blend in with the stem. Tie the stick loosely to the stem with string.

Like other bulbs, lily foliage should be allowed to mature and die back without interference. Because dying foliage leaves blank spaces in the garden in early- to mid-summer, plant annuals in the spring at the base of the lily stems. By the time the lilies fade, the annuals will be at their best.

Cut lilies can last a week or more indoors. Because the stem and foliage produce food for the bulb for the following year's bloom, cut only as much stem as you need to support them in a vase. To avoid staining your clothing or furniture from the heavy pollen on lily blossoms, clip the stamens off before arranging a bouquet.

The Mid-Century Hybrids, such as the Enchantment lily at *right,* also make excellent potted plants. After blossoms fade, plant bulbs in the ground.

FAVORITE VARIETIES

■ Today's hybrid lilies are hardier and more disease-resistant than the strains planted years ago. With the proper selection of lily varieties, you can have blooms from late spring through early fall. For early flowering, select varieties from among the Asiatic, Mid-Century, Martagon, and Bellingham hybrids. In midsummer, the Aurelian Hybrids, such as Pink Perfection and Golden Splendor, come into bloom. The Imperial strains finish up the lily season. Popular lily species include the Martagon lily, the Madonna lily, and the regal lily. Martagon lilies bloom in early summer, followed by the Madonnas. The regal lilies bloom in midsummer.

Summer Bulbs

Summer-blooming bulbs (which actually can be bulbs, tubers, rhizomes, roots, or corms) are less hardy than their springtime cousins. Because they are sensitive to freezing temperatures, such tender bulbs as caladium, dahlia, tuberous begonia, canna lily, calla lily, and gladiolus should be planted in the spring and dug up and stored each fall.

Fancy-leaved caladiums (*right*) are popular for their color-splashed, heart-shaped foliage. Serving double duty, these tender bulbs grow well either in the ground or in planters. Caladiums are bright performers in shady areas, but they're more vibrant when grown in partial sunlight. Choose among combinations of bright red, green, pink, silver, and white.

The exotic canna lily grows 6 feet tall, and produces attractive bronze or green foliage and large blossoms in red, orange, salmon, apricot, coral, pink, yellow, and white. New canna hybrids grow only about half as tall. Best used as accents, cannas need full sunlight.

Gladiolus make spectacular cut flowers. Their dramatic solid and two-toned flower spikes can be grown en masse in a special cutting garden, or in a mixed border with annuals and perennials. Gladiolus bloom 2 to 3 months after they're planted. Keep the garden in full flower by planting them in succession every two weeks. Glads fall over easily, so you may need to stake them. Use inconspicuous bamboo stakes tied with string to support the plants' stems and swordlike, vertical foliage.

SUMMER BULBS IN THE LANDSCAPE

Versatile and easy to care for, summer bulbs will fit anywhere in your garden. Careful planning at planting time will reward you with color all summer.

Dahlias offer an almost unlimited selection of heights, colors, and flower styles, and bloom willingly without being coddled. Their flowers cover the color spectrum, blooming in every shade but blue. Blossom types include single, peony, anemone, cactus, ball, and pompon. Tall, standard dahlias reach 6 feet or more and need staking. Newer dwarf varieties also are available that require no staking, making them ideal bedding plants. Dahlias are most often grown from tubers, but may also be started from seed.

Tuberous begonias flourish in shady areas. Different blossom shapes resemble a rose, camellia, or carnation. Available in both single and double forms, the blooms are up to 10 inches across, and come in white, pink, red, orange, yellow, or salmon; often, they are edged with a contrasting color.

Calla lilies, often grown as houseplants, also do well outdoors in partial shade. Their funnel-shaped pink, yellow, or white flowers bloom over handsome green or spotted foliage 8 weeks after they're planted.

Perfect for shady areas, tuberous begonias can be planted in pots (*above*) to brighten a drab corner on your deck or patio. Trailing types are tailor-made for hanging baskets. Plant tubers 1 inch deep in all-purpose potting soil.

Dahlias look striking in a bed of their own or scattered with annuals and perennials in a mixed flower border. The single-flowered types at *left* bloom with chrysanthemums in the fall when most other flower borders have little or no color.

Caladiums will grow as vigorously in containers as they do in the ground. On the shady patio *opposite*, their variegated foliage blends with potted marigolds and wax begonias to set a colorful stage for relaxing with a good book.

CARE AND MAINTENANCE

Like all bulbs, summer-flowering bulbs require a soil with excellent drainage. Before planting each spring, spade in organic matter as you prepare the soil (see *Soil*, page 8). Work the soil several inches deeper than the planting depth for the bulb.

STARTING BULBS INDOORS

■ While most summer bulbs can be planted directly outdoors in the spring, some types—including tuberous begonia, caladium, and calla lily—benefit from a 4- to 6-week head start indoors. For best results, plant the bulbs in a box or flat filled with an equal mixture of spaghnum peat moss and perlite. Set the box in a warm spot with bright indirect light. After all danger of frost is past, transplant the bulbs outdoors and water thoroughly.

WATERING

■ Water summer bulbs deeply and often. To prolong bloom time and keep disease to a minimum, avoid getting foliage and flowers wet. A mulch of organic material about 2 to 3 inches thick will help conserve moisture and keep roots cool when temperatures climb. All summer bulbs benefit from heavy feeding with a balanced fertilizer.

WINTER STORAGE

■ Because summer bulbs can't withstand cold temperatures, lift them from the ground each fall and store indoors in a dry, cool area over winter. Dig up tuberous begonias before the first expected fall frost. Other bulbs should remain in the ground until the foliage is blackened by frost. Be careful when digging not to cut or damage the roots, corms, tubers, or bulbs.

After digging up bulbs, wash off as much of the soil as possible with a gentle spray of water, and dry them in a sunny spot for several days. Follow these guidelines for storage:

Caladium: Place in a box or plastic bag of dry vermiculite, sphagnum peat moss, or sawdust; store at 60 degrees.

Canna: Dust with a fungicide and store, stem side down, at 45 to 50 degrees in any dry packing material.

Gladiolus: Store corms in mesh bags or old pantyhose, hung from the ceiling in a 35- to 40-degree room.

Dahlia: Allow to dry only slightly and store in a box or plastic bag filled with dry sphagnum peat moss or vermiculite at 35 to 40 degrees. Check bulbs frequently during the winter. If the roots start to shrivel, add a little water; if they start to grow (a sign that they're too

To produce large dahlia flowers, clip off side buds and allow only the center bud (*below*) to develop. This is known as "disbudding."

moist), open the container to let them dry out a little.

Tuberous begonia: Store in any dry packing material at 45 to 60 degrees.

Calla: Store in any dry packing material at 45 to 55 degrees.

Most other bulbs like a dry spot and a temperature around 50 to 60 degrees.

DIVIDING

■ If your summer bulbs need dividing, do it in spring just prior to planting. Cut roots and tubers with a sharp knife, making sure that each division contains at least one growing shoot or eye. True bulbs and corms produce offsets called bulblets or cormels, which can be pulled from the parent and planted separately. They may not bloom during their first year of growth, but in time they will mature to full size.

To produce compact, stockier dahlia plants with more flowers, pinch out the growing tip during the first 4 to 6 weeks.

Canna rhizomes should have at least two growing eyes. Lay them flat in the planting hole so the growing tip rests 1 inch below the soil line. Plant dwarf types 1 foot apart; standard types, 2 feet.

Plant dahlia tubers 4 inches deep, setting them flat in the planting hole. Tall dahlias need support. Drive a stake near the plant at planting time and tie the stem to the stake as it grows.

Gladiolus should be planted in clumps of four or more. Plant large corms 6 inches deep, and smaller ones 2 to 4 inches deep. Set stakes around the clump at planting time if stems need support.

1 Start tuberous begonias 4 to 6 weeks before the last expected frost. Plant the tubers, round side down, 1 inch deep, in potting soil. Overwatering will make tubers rot instead of sprout.

2 Grow in bright indirect light in a warm (65 degrees) spot. Move the pots outdoors when tops are about 3 inches tall and all danger of frost is past.

3 In summer, keep soil evenly moist; mist the foliage when the weather is very hot. Fertilize every week or two with a soluble plant food to produce an array of colorful blooms all season long.

164

VEGETABLES AND HERBS

Homegrown foods, ripened in the sunshine, really do taste better than those that are store-bought. You'll put more vegetables and herbs on the dinner table when you have a big crop of them waiting to be harvested in your backyard. Fresh produce will give your menus a nutritional boost and expose family members to fresh new tastes. What's more, growing vegetables and herbs is an easy and rewarding activity that the whole family can enjoy. There aren't any mysteries to growing your own food—all you need to know are a few basics.

VEGETABLES IN THE LANDSCAPE

With some planning and a little patience, your vegetable garden can become the most eye-appealing element in your landscape. In fact, a neatly groomed vegetable garden can be just as beautiful as a rose garden or perennial border (and certainly tastes better).

HOW TO GET STARTED

■ Vegetables aren't fussy. Their needs are really pretty basic: lots of sunshine, fertile soil, moisture, and a kind hand now and then when weeds or insect pests try to take over. A vegetable garden needn't require a lot of work, either. With early planning and some laborsaving techniques like mulching, wide-row planting, and drip irrigation, you can relax once the rush of spring planting is over. A daily trip to the garden to check your crops' progress and to pull a few weeds is the only summer gardening chore you'll have.

When you're planning your garden, look for a site that gets at least 6 to 8 hours of direct sunlight a day. A level spot is best, but even a steep slope can be tamed with terraces cut into the hillside. Don't locate your garden under trees or near tall, established shrubs. These plants will keep your vegetables from getting sunshine, and their extensive root systems will rob your crops of nutrients and moisture.

SOIL PREPARATION

■ After you've selected your garden spot, it's time to improve soil quality. Even the best soils can stand improvement, so don't skimp when it comes to soil preparation. To get a good indication of your soil's needs, take soil samples and have them analyzed by your extension service, county agent, garden center, or nursery.

Clear the area of branches, stones, and other debris. Strip the sod if you're starting in a grassy area. Compost, rotting leaves, straw (be sure it's weed-free), and manure are all excellent soil amendments. Peat moss, bone meal, dehydrated manures, and cottonseed meal are a few other amendments you can use, depending on the results of your soil test. Till everything under and rake smooth the surface of the garden.

AUTOMATIC WATERING

■ To eliminate watering chores, you may want to install a drip irrigation system after your vegetables are up and growing. Drip systems come in a variety of styles, but they all work on the same principle. Water is delivered in small quantities under low pressure directly to where it does the most good—the root zones of the plants.

Raised beds (*left*) can enhance your home's landscape. You can learn a lot from demonstration gardens. The one at *right* is in St. Louis.

VEGETABLES IN THE LANDSCAPE

Good soil conditioning is the key to the success of the well-planned 40x100-foot seaside garden at *right.* In fall, the gardener spreads several inches of seaweed and rotted poultry manure over the top of the garden and allows it to decompose. In the early spring, all of this organic matter is turned under with a rotary tiller.

When the crops are up and growing, the soil around them is kept cool and moist with a thick mulch of salt hay. Every time a crop is harvested during the growing season, the soil is turned over before another crop is planted. Weeds, which rob the soil of nutrients and moisture, are pulled whenever they appear. Paths, too, are cultivated to keep weeds from getting a foothold.

The magnificent raised-bed garden at *right* is more than just a lush collection of vegetables and flowers. It's also a glorious spot for summer picnics and family get-togethers. The paths between the beds and the patio in the center of the garden are all maintenance-free because they're covered with black plastic topped with a thick layer of pea gravel. There are eight beds in all, four 8x50 feet and four 6x6 feet, which are contained in treated hemlock boards.

To keep the flowers in shape, they're fed a commercial slow-release 14-14-14 mixture of nitrogen, phosphorus, and potassium. Vegetables get a mix of seaweed powder and water, sprayed on their leaves at regular intervals.

For colonial gardeners (*opposite*), a vegetable garden was a necessity.

VEGETABLE GARDEN PLANNING

Once the grip of winter is broken, nothing can stop the force of spring—not even a procrastinating gardener who fails to put growing plans in order. In no time, the soil will be ready for preparation as the threat of frost fades. If proper plans aren't made beforehand, spring can turn into a race for time instead of a season of joy and expectation.

ARMCHAIR PLANNING

■ The first step is to sit down and list the vegetables you want to grow. Be sure to take into account the likes and dislikes of the rest of the family so you're not left with piles of unwanted produce. Then consider some of the space-saving and yield-boosting gardening techniques, such as companion planting, succession planting, intercropping, and second-cropping (see Vegetable Techniques, *page 172*). If this is your first garden, you may have to brave the cold to measure the actual space available for your vegetable crops.

Be as accurate as possible. It may require some extra calculations, but you can save considerable money and time by knowing exactly how much space you have to work with. Then transfer your measurements to a sheet of graph paper so that the sketch matches—to the inch—what you have outside. All that remains is to mark the location of the rows and the vegetables that will occupy them. To avoid midsummer gaps in your garden, plan to replace harvested vegetables with second crops. And also indicate what varieties you plan to squeeze in between rows of other vegetables.

WHEN TO PLANT

■ Proper timing is critical to successful gardening. There are long-season and short-season vegetables, and crops that do better in cooler spring temperatures or warmer summer temperatures.

Long-season crops are those that take the entire season to grow, flower, and produce mature fruit. Cantaloupe, watermelon, winter squash, potato, tomato, corn, cucumber, pumpkin, pepper, and eggplant fall into this category. Short-season vegetables practically explode out of the ground, which means you can plant several times within a single season. Radishes, beans, lettuces, beets, and carrots can be sown and harvested before the season is half over.

Cool-season crops can be planted as early in the spring as you can work the soil. These crops include radish, asparagus, beet, broccoli, Brussels sprouts, cabbage, carrot, cauliflower, celery, Swiss chard, chive, leek, lettuce, onion, parsley, parsnip, pea, potato, rhubarb, spinach, and turnip.

Warm-season crops must be planted after the threat of frost has passed. Those that need warmer temperatures include beans (green and lima), corn, cucumber, eggplant, cantaloupe, pepper, pumpkin, summer squash, winter squash, tomato, and watermelon.

KEEPING RECORDS

■ Because your memory may fade over winter, it's a good idea to keep written records of what you planted and how you did it. Simply note the crops and varieties you grew, and when and how much you planted and harvested. Re-member to leave ample space for your own comments. Keeping track of the varieties you grow will give you the chance to experiment with different varieties. The record of planting dates will give you a clear idea of when to plant next time around.

RAISED-BED GARDENING

■ One popular method that increases yields in small gardens is raised-bed gardening. This system (*right*) works on the principle that deeply dug, fertile soil will allow you to plant more crops in a smaller amount of space.

A raised-bed garden can be any length, but should be no more than five feet wide to let you reach in from either side. First, remove topsoil by digging trenches about 12 inches wide and 12 inches deep. Loosen the subsoil, then mound the topsoil on top. Your finished bed should be four to six inches higher than ground level. Taper sides so rainfall won't wash soil away. Plant seeds in wide bands instead of in individual rows.

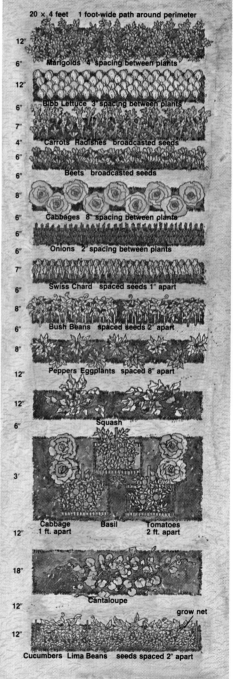

20 × 4 feet   1 foot-wide path around perimeter

12″

6″ Marigolds 4″ spacing between plants

12″

6″ Bibb Lettuce 3″ spacing between plants

7″

4″ Carrots Radishes broadcasted seeds

6″

6″ Beets broadcasted seeds

8″

6″ Cabbages 8″ spacing between plants

6″

6″ Onions 2″ spacing between plants

7″

6″ Swiss Chard spaced seeds 1″ apart

8″

6″ Bush Beans spaced seeds 2″ apart

8″

12″ Peppers Eggplants spaced 8″ apart

12″

6″ Squash

3′

Cabbage   Basil   Tomatoes
12″ 1 ft. apart   2 ft. apart

18″

Cantaloupe

12″   grow net

12″

Cucumbers Lima Beans   seeds spaced 2″ apart

VEGETABLE TECHNIQUES

DOUBLE CROPPING

■ Even if you have an acre of garden space, it's still wise to double up plantings. You'll get twice the harvest with little increase in work. Onions to be used as scallions can be set among cabbage, broccoli, cauliflower, or Brussels sprouts plants. Radishes can be sown with slower germinating carrots. Radishes sprout quickly and prevent weed growth. When radishes are ready to harvest, the carrots can take over. Beets and broccoli also are a good combination. Beets grow rapidly in spring while broccoli is getting established.

The onions and carrots in the garden at *right* can be harvested while still small, leaving space for the lettuce. Or, harvest the carrots and lettuce and allow the onions to develop fully.

COVER CROPPING

■ Cover crops add vital nutrients to the soil, improve drainage, and keep weed growth choked out on fallow areas. Annual rye grass, one of the most popular cover crops, is usually planted in the fall after all the vegetables are harvested. The grass grows quickly during wet, cool fall weather and dies down when the soil freezes. In spring, till the grass under before planting time.

Cover crops are useful in midsummer, too. After cool-weather crops die, cover crops like buckwheat (*right*) can be sown to fill in empty spaces. Or, use vegetables like peas and beans as cover crops in the spring and summer and get a harvest before you till the plants under to add organic matter.

VERTICAL GARDENING

■ If you're short on growing room, try vertical gardening. A sunny section of chain-link or woven-wire fence can support a big crop of vegetables. Climbing peas, pole beans, melons, pumpkins, and squash will grow on vertical supports. Melons and squash fruits need sling supports to keep the weight from pulling vines off the fence. Improvise slings of net and tie to the fence.

Another space-saving trick is to grow vine crops on trellises (*left*) made of lath stakes or bamboo poles. Plant seeds at the base and get ready to harvest a triple-size crop. If you have a surplus of shrub prunings, pile them up and let beans ramble over the stack. If you have a long growing season, plant an early pea crop and a late bean crop.

WIDE-ROW GARDENING

■ One of the best ways to increase yield without tilling up more space is to garden in wide rows. Wide-row gardening works on the principle that plants sown close together (*left*) produce up to four times as much harvest as the same area planted single file. Individual plants might not produce as much as when they're spaced according to seed pack instructions, but on the whole, volume of production will be much greater.

Wide-row gardening eliminates a lot of weeding, because vegetables grow thickly to choke out weeds. When you grow cool-weather crops like lettuce, spinach, and peas in the wide-row system, you'll also be extending your harvest, because the plants will shade each other during hot weather.

173

Small-Space Gardens

Truly successful gardeners plan their vegetable gardens to get two or three major harvests in one season. When one crop matures, another is planted. And, whenever possible, two crops with different maturity dates are planted together for a staggered harvest.

PLANT EVERY SQUARE INCH

■ To ensure continuous production, keep garden space filled. The garden at *right* is a perfect example of multiple-harvest planning. The large 10x16-foot bed is planted with cool-season crops in early April—spinach, lettuce, beets, radishes, carrots, onions, and peas. By late May, most of these crops have been harvested and the warm-weather crops planted, including beans, cucumbers, cantaloupes, and more carrots. Cool-season crops that remain have warm-weather crops planted around them.

The 5x8 bed is planted with long-maturing crops. Here, vegetables like eggplant, broccoli, cabbage, and corn grow undisturbed until harvest. Even these long-season vegetables are replaced in late summer with lettuce, radish, and kale for late-fall harvest.

PREPARE SOIL CAREFULLY

■ You'll need to prepare your soil well to keep your garden in constant production, as shown at *right.* First, both beds were staked out and 1x8 sideboards installed. Then, the beds were dug to a depth of 4 inches and layers of compost, manure, sawdust, and soil were added until the soil level reached the top of the boards. Lengths of 2x4s set over the beds let this gardener tend the crops without walking on the soil.

RAISED-BED GARDENS

One of the best raised-bed gardens in the country belongs to Peter and Sylvia Chan. To improve their soil and to beef up vegetable production, the Chans dug a system of raised beds similar to those used in southern China. Their garden (*opposite*) measures 50x25 feet and consists of ten 25-foot-long raised beds. The beds are four feet wide and separated by foot-wide paths.

The Chans use a small grow-light unit set up in their study to help start vegetables like broccoli, lettuce, beans, kohlrabi, and spinach. They sow seeds three to five weeks before planting in the garden. When the seedlings are about an inch high, the tiny plants are moved into individual two-inch pots. Once established in the pots, the plants are moved outdoors into a portable cold frame to harden off.

After a week or so in the cold frames, the seedlings are moved into their permanent locations in the garden. Peter adds a little dehydrated chicken manure to the bottom of each hole and tops the fertilizer with a thin layer of soil to prevent damage to the seedling's roots.

Later, as the crops grow, Peter feeds them once a week with a diluted solution of manure tea. Crops like peas and beans are sown directly into the beds with a little dehydrated chicken manure in the bottom of each furrow.

GETTING STARTED

■ Soil preparation is the key to this garden's success. First, the location of each bed is marked off with twine. Then, a sharp spade is used to turn the soil in the bed to a depth of ten or 12 inches. As the soil is turned, rocks, weeds, grass, and other debris are removed. After digging, the level of the bed is higher than the area around it because the soil is in a well-worked state; no new soil has been added. The sides of the beds are tapered so heavy rainfall won't wash the soil away.

All this might sound like a lot of work, but remember that once a raised bed is established, it's permanent. You needn't redig or till the garden every spring, as you must do with a flat garden. Raised beds also dry out more quickly in the spring, giving you a head start on the season. Raised beds do, however, require more frequent watering than traditional flat gardens.

In the fall, Peter and Sylvia dig a trench down the center of each raised bed. They then spread compost and organic matter from their compost bin and refill the trenches with soil. In the spring the Chans rake the beds smooth.

To save space, the Chans train pole beans and peas up lightweight wooden supports made from lengths of 1x2 and 2x2 lumber. Each support is portable and fits over an entire raised bed.

GETTING STARTED

A seed holds an incredible life force. When conditions are right, the seed bursts, sending forth an embryo root and stem. Each time, the same thing happens with mind-boggling regularity. But the key to the process is to give the right seed the right conditions— which is the gardener's job.

Good germination needs moisture and warmth. Ideally, the temperature should be between 70 and 80 degrees Fahrenheit. Moisture is necessary to soften hard seed shells and provide nutrients for developing roots.

Naturally, soil conditions are important for germination, too. After you've turned and fortified the soil with lime, fertilizer, and organic matter (see Soil, *pages 8 and 9*), mark the exact location of the row. Place small stakes at each end, and stretch twine between them. Then, using the twine as a guide, dig a furrow with the corner of a hoe blade (or the handle end if a shallow furrow is needed). The idea is to plant seed at the right depth. The deeper you go, the cooler the soil temperature; but the shallower the furrow, the drier the soil. A good rule of thumb is to plant seed at a depth equal to four times its diameter.

SOWING SEEDS OUTDOORS

■ If seeds are small, take a pinch between thumb and index finger and sow by rubbing fingers together over the furrow. Larger seeds can be planted individually. Cover seed with soil and tamp gently with your hand or the back of your hoe blade. Remove twine and mark the row with an empty seed packet or plant label. Water gently but thoroughly; if a dry spell occurs, keep soil moist by placing a thin mulch of dried lawn clippings or partially rotted compost over the row.

PLANTING SEEDLINGS

■ When setting out young seedlings, mark rows with twine and dig holes at recommended intervals. Fill holes with water, allow them to drain, and set in plants after placing foil or paper collars around stems to prevent cutworm damage. Then fill in soil, being sure to eliminate unwanted air spaces, and tamp gently. If plants appear to be suffering from the intense sun, shade can be supplied by placing shields made of brush or small boards next to each plant. Water frequently.

For information about starting seeds indoors, see page 92.

When you start plants from seeds outdoors, it may be necessary to thin out some plants. Use scissors or shears and cut the stem at ground level. Pulling can damage neighboring seedlings.

EXTENDING THE SEASON

Growing vegetables outdoors year-round is easy, even in northern climates, when you extend your growing season with a cloche or cold frame. These structures are designed to take full advantage of the sun's rays so that you can start gardening earlier in the spring and continue to produce harvests well after the first frost. In some cases, you may even be able to grow crops in midwinter when the rest of the garden is covered with snow.

For example, the cold frame *opposite* has a double-glazed fiberglass top that's curved to take full advantage of the sun's rays and allow plenty of growing room for the crops. A 55-gallon drum, painted black and filled with water, absorbs heat from the sun and helps keep temperatures stable.

Wall O' Water caps let you protect individual plants. Filled with water, tubes capture heat from the sun during the day and stay warm as evening temperatures drop.

This portable cold frame has a 3x4-foot frame made of 1x2 redwood lumber. Clear plastic sheeting forms the walls. A plastic cover can be unrolled over the top.

Newly germinated celery plants are sheltered by panes of glass held together with aluminum clips. Celery is slow to germinate; this method accelerates growth by warming the soil.

Start crops like broccoli and cauliflower under row-long plastic tents. Each tent has two sheets of thick plastic—one clear and one black. The black plastic absorbs heat and helps keep the soil warm.

This cold frame is made from railroad ties and old windows. When the temperature inside rises, the window is propped up. When the temperature cools, the window is closed.

CARE AND MAINTENANCE

The quality and quantity of the vegetables you grow depends on whether the soil offers plants a good root environment and good nutrition. For the plant to thrive, the roots must penetrate the soil easily and draw adequate food.

If you already have a vegetable garden, your soil is probably in good shape. However, if you are breaking new ground, your soil may be less than ideal the first year.

Turn or till the soil a full-spade depth. Add all the organic material you can find and turn it under. Leaves, grass clippings, well-rotted manure, straw, compost, and leafy kitchen scraps are good organic soil improvers.

If your soil is acidic, scatter lime over the surface before digging. For heavy clay soil, try gypsum to modify the soil and make it easier to work.

After you've dug the soil and raked it roughly level, sprinkle the surface with a vegetable garden fertilizer. Be sure to follow the directions on the bag. After scattering fertilizer, rake it into the top two inches of soil.

The soil will be in the best condition for planting if you turn it in late fall—and you'll also lighten your gardening chores for the following spring.

WATERING
■ One inch of gentle rain each week during the growing season is every gardener's dream. However, this rarely happens. Don't be frugal when watering early in the season because roots are shallow and the plants will not develop optimally and bear fruit if the soil is allowed to dry out.

MULCHING
■ To save work, time, and money, mulch your garden in late spring. This protective cover insulates the soil against the heat of the summer sun, protects it from the drying winds, and all but eliminates weeds. Once the mulch is applied, you don't have to hoe between the rows, and, during most growing seasons, you have to water about one-third as often. And, as the organic mulches decay, they improve the soil. Wait to mulch until after the soil has warmed and before the weeds have started growing.

You can choose between organic mulches (straw, peat moss, sawdust, dry manure, and bark chips) and inorganic mulches (paper and polyethylene film). Inorganics work for vining crops like melons and squash.

A tomato plant can send out roots from any part of its stem. For extra-leggy plants, bury the entire stem lengthwise in a trench under the soil surface.

Cutworms feed on seedling stems. To combat these pests, wrap the bottom inch or two with a newspaper or foil collar extending just below the soil. Remove collar after plants are established.

For continuous harvests, vegetables like beans and peas should be picked often; during the peak of the season, you may harvest daily. Pods should be picked before seeds swell to cause visible bulges.

To blanch cauliflower heads, use twine or a rubber band to tie plant leaves over the top of developing head. This will shade the head, keeping it compact and white.

Some cool-weather crops like lettuce and spinach will bolt (go to seed) during hot weather. When this happens, pull plants and throw them on your compost pile. Choose more heat-resistant varieties.

Harvest broccoli when heads are tight and compact, usually when they're about 5 inches in diameter. If you wait too long, the head will produce small yellow flowers and be inedible. After you cut the main head, leave the plant intact. In a few weeks, smaller heads (*above*) will develop from side shoots along the plant's stem. Cut these smaller heads when they're about an inch or two across.

HERBS

Today's gardeners enjoy herbs for their fragrance, flavor, and rich ancestry. Many gardeners devote space to herbs simply because they are easy to grow. Herbs will thrive in places where other plants generally won't, demanding only sun or partial sun, and well-drained soil.

Feature your favorites in a separate herb garden, either formally to imitate a stately royal garden, or informally to create a natural thicket in your backyard. Or tuck a few herbs into existing gardens to provide a lush backdrop for flowers or a border around vegetables.

Herbs traditionally are planted in geometric shapes, with plants grouped according to flavor or fragrance. One of the simplest designs consists of four beds with intersecting paths. The design can be modified by enlarging the beds and adding more paths.

Popular cooking herbs include savory, basil, spearmint, chives, dill, oregano, parsley, and sage. Mint, scented geranium, thyme, lavender, and rosemary are favorite fragrant types. Cold-sensitive herbs can be grown in pots, then taken indoors for the winter.

CARE AND MAINTENANCE

Herbs are easy to grow if you meet a few basic requirements. Most herbs do best in the sun. Herbs' essential oils, which account for their flavor and fragrance, are produced in the greatest quantities when the herbs receive 6 to 8 hours of sunshine a day.

Most herbs will thrive in any good garden loam. A soil pH of neutral to slightly alkaline, which can be corrected with lime, is best. Well-drained soil is essential; improve poor-draining soils with sand and organic material. Once established, most herbs are extremely hardy. Fertilize heavily harvested herbs such as basil, chives, and parsley. Too much water and/or fertilizer will produce lush foliage but low oil content and, therefore, you'll harvest little flavor or fragrance.

Weeds are undoubtedly an herb's worst enemy. If not controlled from the start, weeds will choke out the young plants. A friable soil prior to planting will discourage competition at the start. For extra protection, spread two or three inches of mulch around your herbs after they are established.

The leaves or tops of most herbs should be harvested when fresh and green—just before full bloom. Cut plants after morning dew evaporates, and hang upside down.

Another drying method is to spread the herbs on wire racks until they're completely dry. Crumble and store the herbs in airtight containers.

ROSES

Throughout history, no one flower has been more cherished, revered, or steeped in tradition than the rose. In the landscape, this timeless favorite offers permanence. Unlike annual flowers, which endure for a season and must be planted again each succeeding spring, the rose rewards you year after year with fresh, fragrant blooms. Consider the many ways you can use roses to enhance your property—as a foundation planting; as a border along a fence, a walk, or a vegetable garden; massed for a wall of bloom by a deck; potted up for a spot of color on a patio; or climbing a trellis. A traditional symbol of love, roses gracefully repay a gardener's devotion with their elegant beauty.

ROSES IN THE LANDSCAPE

Every garden has room for at least one rosebush, if not more. In a shrub border, try mixing a few old-fashioned roses with spring-blooming plants like forsythia and lilac. As the flowers of the shrubs begin to fade, the roses will burst into bloom, extending the color show well into the summer.

MIXED OR ALONE
■ Perennial flowers and roses go well together, too. The roses provide continuous color while the various perennials go in and out of bloom. In the garden corner *below, right,* Olé, a fiery red grandiflora, blooms harmoniously alongside cranesbill geranium, sedum, snapdragon, lily, iris, statice, and delphinium. For perennial borders too small to accommodate the taller roses, you can add lots of color by edging the garden with miniature roses.

Climbers and ramblers are excellent for camouflaging unsightly buildings, fences, and walls. These vigorous plants grow rapidly and will completely cover the worst eyesore with blooms in just a season or two. Large, traditional rose arbors (*opposite*) are always impressive. Where space is tight, you can get the same effect with a modest arbor over your garden path. Sometimes just one climber in full bloom can be more effective than a whole border of flowers.

Roses provide a beautiful, fragrant border along a deck or patio. Choose white or light-colored roses if you use the patio at night, because they'll show up better in the dark.

Some roses will sprawl over the ground and act as a colorful ground cover. Similar types can be planted atop stone fences or retaining walls and allowed to spill to the ground.

Roses grown in containers are popular for small city gardens and balconies. Use compact minis and floribundas for best results. Move the pots around to create different effects.

HEDGE ROSES
■ A rose hedge will add elegance to your yard. Tall shrubs make excellent privacy screens. Medium-size floribundas divide property without giving that boxed-in look. Low-growing minis and polyanthas can separate areas with a bright strip of color.

When planting a hedge of roses, stick to one basic color and size, and space the plants closely together to ensure dense growth. If you're planting roses along a walkway or patio, set them far enough back so passersby will not be caught by thorns.

Mini-tree roses (*above*) bring a touch of elegance to your garden. These stately attention grabbers stand about 2 feet tall and look terrific set along a low garden wall.

ROSE CLASSIFICATION

Roses are classified into several categories based on a number of plant and blossom characteristics, including size, shape, and form. Classifications include the hybrid tea, floribunda, grandiflora, miniature, climber, old garden rose, shrub, and polyantha. A study of these rose classifications is a lesson in their history as well, from the oldest old garden rose, through a continuous series of developments and hybridizations, to present-day varieties.

The old garden rose class is divided into several subclasses, including alba, Bourbon, centifolia, China, Damask, Gallica, hybrid foetida, hybrid perpetual, hybrid spinosissima, moss, noisette, species, and tea. The shrub rose category includes eglanteria, hybrid moyesi, hybrid rugosa, kordesi, musk, and the shrub roses.

The grandiflora is a hybrid. From the hybrid tea, it inherits flower form and long cutting stems; from the floribunda, it receives hardiness and continuous clusters of bloom.

Any rose class existing before 1867 qualifies as an old garden rose. Old garden roses stand on their own virtues: hardiness, fragrance, and low maintenance.

As the buds of the hybrid tea open, they reveal swirls of petals and elegant, high-centered blooms on 2- to 5-foot-tall stems. Many emit the famous rose fragrance and are a perfect choice to fill a vase.

The floribunda is a cross between the classic hybrid tea and the polyantha, with its abundant sprays. Hardier and bushier than hybrid teas, floribundas make good landscape plants.

Few plants are as tough and tolerant of neglect and poor growing conditions as shrub roses. They vary in height from low-growing ground covers to taller types used in hedges.

ROSE CLASSIFICATION

Consider height, hardiness, and climatic needs when you select roses. Colors and forms should complement your landscape, as well as your taste.

THE AMERICAN ROSE SOCIETY
■ To make choosing roses easier, the American Rose Society, an international association of amateur and professional rose growers, has classified all roses into seventeen color categories: white, medium yellow, deep yellow, yellow blend, apricot blend, orange and orange blend, orange-red, light pink, medium pink, pink blend, medium red, dark red, red blend, mauve, russet, and mauve blend.

Each year, members of the American Rose Society establish ratings for commercially available rose varieties. This system gives a numerical rating from 0.0 to 10.0 for all roses. For a copy of these published ratings, send $1 to *Handbook for Selecting Roses*, Box 30000, Shreveport, LA 71130.

ALL-AMERICA ROSES
■ When choosing varieties for your rose garden, look also to the winners of the annual All-America Rose Selections (AARS) award. This organization, in existence since 1938, tests new roses to determine which are worthy of recommendation to American gardeners.

The AARS grows rose plants in over two dozen test gardens across the country so that each rose is exposed to a variety of soil and climatic conditions. Testing criteria include habit, vigor, hardiness, disease resistance, frequency of bloom, foliage, flower form, substance, opening and finishing color, fragrance, and novelty. After a two-year test, varieties with the highest scores receive the AARS highly acclaimed stamp of approval.

PERSONAL PREFERENCE
■ The final variety selection you make will depend on how you want to use the rose. If you want to plant a rose in a container, look for one that is compact and floriferous. A small container will best suit a miniature or a polyantha, and a larger container will accommodate one floribunda. For a hedge, choose a floribunda. Miniature roses are perfect for low edgings, and shrub roses work well for large screens. Along fences, try climbers, which also do well against arbors and trellises. Flower arranging enthusiasts should consider planting fragrant hybrid teas or grandifloras.

A miniature rose is a tiny reproduction of a full-size rose, with flowers, leaves, and stems shrunken in proportionate size. Plants range from 3 to 4 inches high to 18 to 24 inches tall.

Any bush rose variety can be grafted to an understock stem to create a tree rose. Tree roses can accent a bed, decorate a patio, or add distinction to any planting. They're ideal for a formal garden.

Climbers have long, pliable canes that can be trained on supports. These hardy plants produce loose clusters of large flowers. Climbing sports have the same flowers as their parents but are not as hardy.

HOW TO PLANT A ROSE

When should you plant roses? Bare-root roses should be planted at times when they are dormant and the ground is not frozen. In warm areas, this is in late winter. Where winter temperatures do not go below 0° Fahrenheit, planting may be done in early spring or late fall. In areas of extreme cold, roses should be planted only in the spring. Where possible, plant in fall, because roots will grow for much of the winter, leading to strong top growth in spring.

BARE-ROOT ROSES

■ Bare-root roses should be planted as soon as possible after you receive them. If you won't have a chance to plant them for several days, keep them in a cool, dark spot and keep the roots moist by wrapping them in damp newspaper or peat moss. If you can't plant your bare-root roses for several weeks, heel them in by burying the entire plant in a trench in a cool, shaded spot. Planting instructions for bare-root roses are outlined in steps 1 to 5 *opposite*.

CONTAINER ROSES

■ When you buy roses already growing in containers, you can extend the planting season into summer, allowing you to fill in bits of color in the garden where it's needed.

Plant container roses the same way as other containerized shrubs; be sure to carefully remove the container (*right*) before planting, to help ensure fast and strong root growth. Keep roses well-watered, especially in the summertime, until they're established.

PLACING AND SPACING

■ In most climates, hybrid teas, grandifloras, and floribundas should be plant-ed 24 inches apart. Where winters are mild, allow more space; for dense edging or hedging, space a little closer together. Because shrub and old garden roses will grow large, space them up to 4 to 6 feet apart, depending on their mature size. For climbers to be trained horizontally along a fence, allow a distance of 8 to 10 feet between plants. Plant minis from 8 to 18 inches apart depending on their mature size.

Plan ahead when placing roses in your landscape. Because they are permanent features, place them where they can remain indefinitely. Plant roses where they will receive at least 6 hours of direct sun each day; morning sun is preferable so the foliage can dry , which reduces the chances of disease. Where summer heat is intense, place roses where they will get light afternoon shade. Minis and climbers will be happy with a little less sun than their larger cousins, and can be grown in the shade of an ornamental tree. High winds can damage or destroy open flowers. If possible, protect roses from wind by planting by a fence, hedge, or other barrier.

GIVE ROSES A GOOD START

■ A rose is no better than the soil it's planted in, so give extra attention to soil preparation. Soil should be light and rich; improve it by mixing in organic matter such as peat moss, leaf mold, or compost. Heavy clay soils can be loosened with gypsum. Because roses don't like wet feet, improve soil drainage by adding perlite, vermiculite, or sand. The pH for roses should be between 6.0 and 6.5. Correct it with lime or sulfur if needed. Add superphosphate before planting.

KEEP RECORDS

■ A variety label is usually attached with a piece of wire to a cane on a rosebush. Insert the label into the ground near the rose, and keep a separate record of what varieties you plant.

1 Before planting, soak roots of bare-root roses in water overnight to restore lost moisture. Prune back any broken, damaged, or too-long roots.

2 Dig a hole 24 inches deep and wide, and place a mound of soil in the bottom of the hole. Position the bud union so that it is in line with ground level.

3 Backfill the planting hole two-thirds full, add water, and allow to drain. Fill the hole, then mound soil around the canes to keep them moist. Create a well around the mound and keep watered.

4 Roses can be further protected from drying out with a mulch of organic matter. Keep this in place until new growth begins, then wash away carefully with a gentle stream of water.

5 Prune roses back by a third after planting, and remove any dead or broken wood at the same time. This will encourage new, strong canes from the start.

PRUNING ROSES

It may seem like you're taking a step backward to cut away healthy wood from a rose, but it's actually in the rose's best interest. Pruning is necessary to control the size and shape of a plant and to keep it healthy, vigorous, and covered in bloom. If you fail to prune, the rosebush will soon become tall and rangy and produce few good flowers.

TIMING

■ Pruning should be done before the buds break, just after they have begun to swell. Timing will range from mid-winter to mid-spring, depending on your climate. If forsythia blooms in your neighborhood, prune roses when yellow forsythia buds begin to show.

PRUNING TECHNIQUES

■ It's important to use the right tools for the job. A curved-edged pruning shears is better than a straight-edged anvil type, which can crush the stems as it cuts. Use a long-handled lopper or a pruning saw for thick canes.

Prune hybrid teas, floribundas, and grandifloras as illustrated *below right*.

Where winterkill does not force you into a lower pruning height, cut canes to a height of 12 to 18 inches. Floribundas can be left taller and fuller for increased flowering capabilities.

Climbers are pruned as shown *far opposite*. The hybrid perpetuals should have only the oldest canes removed. Prune shrub and old garden roses just to shape them and to remove dead wood. Prune minis to about half of their summer height; shape them according to their use in your landscape. Tree roses are pruned like bush roses, but they must be kept symmetrical. Polyanthas require little pruning. Cut their height by half, and shape; remove dead wood as it appears. Because trimmed canes can be a source for blackspot spores, throw them away immediately after pruning.

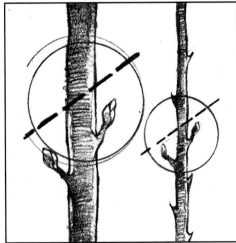

Make all pruning cuts at a 45-degree angle about ¼ inch above a bud and sloping downward, so water runs off. If too much cane is left, it will suffer dieback, a condition where woody parts die.

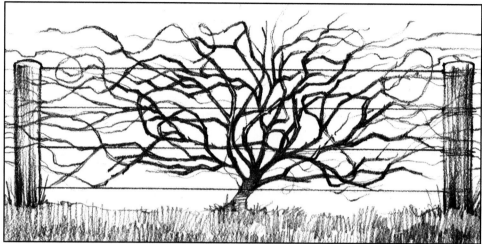

On hybrid teas, cut out dead canes to the bud union, then remove weak, damaged, or diseased wood. Prune to an outside-facing bud to keep the plant open.

Climbers are pruned later than bush roses because they bloom on old wood. Remove dead canes and those that are not contributing to a desirable shape.

Pruning climbers too much in spring only leads to cutting away the flower show. Spend this time training the canes along a fence and securing them with plant ties.

Remove any canes growing into the center, as well as those that crisscross. By this time, there should be several canes left. Save 3 or 4 of the newest and best; remove all others, leaving no stubs.

After a climber has bloomed, remove 2 or 3 of the oldest canes to make room for fresh new growth. Thin out dense growth and shorten the canes of plants that have grown too large.

A rose grows where it is cut, so cut canes back further than you want their final size to be. Climbers will flower optimally if trained horizontally and if laterals are cut back immediately after flowering.

CARE AND MAINTENANCE

If you take care of your roses, they will reward you all summer with beautiful blooms. Proper watering, mulching, fertilizing, and winter protection will help roses survive and flourish.

WATERING

■ With the right amount of water, roses will produce larger, longer-lasting blossoms with better color. One inch of water per week is ideal; use a rain gauge as a guide. During times of extended drought and high temperatures, water more frequently. Sandy soils may need to be watered more often and clay soils less often.

Roses can be watered by subirrigation pipes, soaker hoses laid on the ground, or overhead sprinklers. The method you choose will depend on your garden size and budget. Overhead sprinkling is one of the easiest and least expensive methods; water only in the morning so the leaves will not go through the night wet, which invites fungus problems.

MULCHING

■ In mid-spring, after the ground is warm, apply a 2- to 3-inch layer of mulch around your roses. In the summer, mulch will keep the soil cooler, moister, and more weed-free. As it decomposes, it also will enrich the soil. Left in place all winter, mulch will insulate the soil to help eliminate the threat of plants being heaved out of their resting places when the soil alternately freezes and thaws. Mulched roses will also stay cleaner because the protective covering prevents any soil from splattering the foliage and flowers during watering or rainstorms. Do not allow mulch to come in contact with canes.

Whether you're removing spent blossoms or cutting flowers for bouquets, make a cut at an angle above a 5-leaflet leaf, which is where the new growth will start.

Disbudding will give you one large flower per stem. Remove small buds as they appear around the central flower. On a floribunda, take out the center bud.

Roses should be fed three times a year with a rose fertilizer spread over the root area. Feed after pruning in early spring, just before the first bloom, and two months before the first expected fall frost.

Rose foliage needs regular spraying or dusting to prevent a variety of diseases, such as blackspot and mildew. Treat for aphids, Japanese beetles, and other insect problems as they appear.

WINTER PROTECTION

■ Most roses need protection in areas where winter temperatures regularly drop below 20 degrees Fahrenheit. Fluctuations in temperature, extended periods of severe cold, and harsh, drying winds cause winter dieback. A deep and constant snow cover can't be beat, but you'll probably need to provide additional protection. Shrub, old garden, and miniature roses, however, are relatively hardy and need little protection.

The best rosebush protection is to mound soil over canes to a height of at least 12 inches. Bring soil from another area to avoid exposing delicate feeder roots to cold air. Remove soil mound when growth starts in spring. For extra protection, mulch with wood chips or leaves. Apply mulch after the ground freezes, and carefully remove in spring.

1 Tree roses are particularly vulnerable to cold. They can be brought indoors, buried, or wrapped. To wrap, start by setting four stakes around the plant.

2 Wrap burlap around stakes and tie. This lets air circulate, lowers the chance of disease, and prevents premature growth caused by an interior greenhouse effect.

Where temperatures dip below zero, take climber canes off of supports and secure them on the ground. Cover with leaves or soil. You can also leave canes in place and wrap them with burlap.

Instead of using soil around canes, you can also mound up other organic materials, such as bark chips (*above*). In the spring, remove the material carefully to avoid breaking off new plant growth.

In very cold climates, rose plants need heavy protection. Use a paper, cardboard, plastic, or metal cylinder and fill it with bark, leaves, or newspaper. You can also use plastic foam rose cones.

INSECTS AND DISEASES

INSECT/DISEASE	DESCRIPTION AND TROUBLE SIGNS	CONTROL
Aphids	Aphids, also called plant lice, are tiny but visible green or brown insects that form colonies along flower buds and new shoot growth, starting in mid- to late spring. They harm roses by sucking away their vital juices.	Aphids can be knocked off the plant with a strong stream of water from the garden hose or with a spray of soapy water; or use a commercial insecticide.
Black spot	Black spot, as the name implies, is a fungus disease that causes rounded, black spots to appear on the foliage of rosebushes. Eventually a yellow halo forms around the black spot, then the entire leaf turns yellow and falls off.	When you prune in spring, throw away all clippings—you'll be throwing away a lot of black spot spores with them. Don't water from overhead. Use a commercial fungicide.
Canker	Canker is a fungus disease that causes canes to die. You will usually notice cankers in the early spring at pruning time; a part of the cane will be healthy but above it will be a black, brown, or purple discoloration. Canker usually enters through a wound.	Canker can't be controlled with chemicals, but you can be careful to prevent wounds. In spring, prune all canes to below any sign of canker.
Japanese beetle	Japanese beetles are shiny copper and green beetles that can devastate the entire garden in a short time. They eat holes in the flowers, and, if hungry enough, will eat the foliage. They're particularly attracted to light colored flowers.	If you don't have too many Japanese beetles, you can pick them off by hand and destroy them. Traps work, as does the controlling of grubs in the soil with an insecticide.
Leaf rollers	These tiny caterpillars roll themselves up in the rose foliage and eat through it from the inside out. Another tell-tale sign of these pests is tiny holes in the base of the flower buds.	There are few ways to control them physically, but a commercial insecticide will easily keep them in tow.

INSECT/DISEASE	DESCRIPTION AND TROUBLE SIGNS	CONTROL
Midge	A midge is an insect that is actually a tiny maggot which bores into a rose plant, causing the buds and new shoots to suddenly blacken.	When you see signs of midge, prune out the damaged pieces immediately and discard. Some commercial insecticides will put a stop to midge.
Mildew	When a white powder forms on rosebuds and leaves, you have a case of mildew. It is most prevalent when cool nights follow warm days, or where air circulation is poor. Mildew often causes a serious disfiguration of rose foliage.	If you can plant roses where air circulation is good, you'll eliminate the chances of mildew. A commercial fungicide will work if used as a preventive.
Rust	When the powder on your rosebuds and leaves is orange, you have a disease known as rust. Primarily confined to the West Coast, rust is caused by wet and mild weather.	Before you plant a new rosebush, inspect it carefully for signs of rust and don't plant it if you see any. Control with a commercial fungicide.
Spider mites	You won't be able to see the spider mite, but you will be able to see its devastating effects. It's not an insect, but it does the damage of one. Foliage turns a dull red, and you can see webs in advanced stages. They weaken roses by sucking juices from foliage.	The one thing spider mites can't stand is water, so keep the plants well watered and hose down the undersides of the leaves. Miticide can be used three days apart.
Thrips	If the garden should be in bloom but it isn't, you may have thrips—microscopic insects that bore into the petals and suck juices from the flower. Buds become distorted and brown and will not open.	Since thrips hide in the buds and flowers, cut buds off and destroy them. Insecticides applied to the buds and the ground will keep thrips away.

FRUITS AND BERRIES

Fruit and berry plants will delight you for years with fresh produce. Fruits also are a feast for the eyes in the landscape. Use dwarf or semidwarf fruit trees to define a lot line or screen a pool or patio. Or plant a pair as specimens on either side of your front lawn or walk. Mingle shrub fruits like blueberries, currants, gooseberries, and elderberries with spring-flowering shrubs. Use strawberries as a ground cover, or grow them in containers. Grapes can be trained over an arbor for shade and convenient picking. All of the hardy fruits in this section are easy to grow and take up less space than you might think.

FRUIT IN THE LANDSCAPE

Fruit- and berry-producing plants are more than natural food factories. They also add distinctive colors, shapes, and fragrances to a landscape plan.

The backyard apple orchard *below* is awash with blooms in the spring, offers shady relief in the summer, and bears bushels of fresh produce in late summer and early fall. Even if you don't have plenty of open yard space, you can plant several dwarf fruit trees.

Fruit trees don't always have to be planted in the regimented rows of an orchard to bear fruit. You can use pears, peaches, or dwarf apple varieties as accent plantings near your house. Because fruit trees bloom in the spring, they are perfect mates for foundation and ornamental plants. Keep in mind that some fruits will need companion trees for proper pollination.

POT UP MINIATURE TREES FOR SMALL SPACES
■ Miniature fruit trees are the answer for small yards. These waist-high wonders rarely grow over 6 feet tall, yet they bear only a year or two after planting. Just three years old, the tiny Bonanza peach *opposite* already produces big crops of luscious fruit.

Also called genetic dwarfs, miniature fruit trees are available in peach, nectarine, cherry, apple, apricot, pear, plum, and almond varieties. But don't let the terms "miniature" or "genetic dwarf" fool you. These short, stocky trees develop full-size fruit that's just as delicious as that from taller trees.

Along with being productive and good looking, container-grown miniature fruit trees also are portable. Use them to enhance a bare deck or patio, flank a front door, or team with a collection of potted flowers. For easy moving, install casters on the bottom of the container at planting time. If you live in the Deep South or on the West Coast (wherever winter temperatures remain above 25 degrees F.), you can grow miniature fruit trees in the ground.

Even if they didn't produce fruit, miniature fruit trees would still be a gardener's dream. These stocky charmers never outgrow their positions in the landscape. Pruning chores are minimal and the plants' compact growth habit makes insect and disease control easy.

In the North, container-grown miniature fruit trees need protection during the winter months. After nighttime temperatures begin to drop below 25 degrees F., move your trees into an unheated garage, shed, or porch. Water the container thoroughly and mulch it with a thick layer of leaves or straw.

GROW GRAPES FOR SHADE
■ One excellent way to get shade over a deck or patio is to train grapevines over an arbor. Four varieties of grapes clamber over the deck arbor *opposite.* The elevated plants create an attractive canopy of cool green leaves on hot summer days. At the same time, fruits will get plenty of ventilation, which will reduce the threat of fungus diseases. As young plants develop, tie canes to posts with soft twine or strips of cloth.

SELECTING FRUIT TREES

Your climate plays a big role in helping you select which fruit trees you can grow. Hardy trees, such as apple, need a period of cold for their growth cycle to continue. But tender trees, such as peach, will get nipped in the bud if winter temperatures are too low.

If you're limited on space, plant a semidwarf (12 to 15 feet tall), dwarf (8 to 10 feet tall), or miniature (6 feet tall) variety. These smaller trees will bear the same size fruit as their standard cousins, at an earlier age.

Some fruit trees are self-fruitful, which means blossoms can be fertilized by pollen from blossoms on the same plant. But other types need a little help from neighboring varieties. To ensure proper pollination of your fruit tree, plant a companion variety within 100 feet, so bees can travel between.

Most apples must be cross-pollinated using simultaneously blooming varieties. Golden Delicious and Rome Beauty will self-pollinate.

Pears generally need two varieties to bear fruit. Kieffer and Duchess are the self-pollinating exceptions. Bartlett and Seckel will not pollinate each other.

Although sour cherries are self-pollinating, sweet cherries—such as Lambert, Bing, Napoleon, and Emperor Francis—need a second variety, such as Black Tartarian, for pollination.

All apricot and nectarine varieties are self-fruitful. Most peach varieties are self-fruitful, but a few require a cross-pollinator. J.H. Hale is one peach that must be cross-pollinated.

Most Japanese (red) plums require a second Japanese plum, but Santa Rosa will pollinate itself, and Burbank and Shiro will not cross-pollinate. European (blue) plums are self-pollinating.

CANE AND BUSH FRUITS

Cane and bush fruits are a tasty solution for gardeners who don't have the space for fruit trees. When grown against a fence, berry plants fill otherwise unused space. Before making any selections, ask a local nurseryman which varieties are suitable for your area.

RASPBERRIES
■ Just note the high price of fresh raspberries at the grocery store, and you'll know that this cane fruit is as good as gold. Raspberries were once confined to cold-winter areas, but many newer varieties will thrive in warm regions.

Raspberry varieties fall into two groups: summer-fruiting and everbearing. The summer-fruiting raspberry produces berries on the previous season's canes in early to midsummer. The newer everbearing types bear fruit twice, once in early summer on the previous season's growth, and again in the fall on the current season's growth.

Red and black are the two most common types, but purple and yellow varieties also exist. Red raspberries grow on thorny, erect canes, and black varieties have thorny, arching branches.

BLACKBERRIES
■ Though frequently confused with black raspberries, blackberries are larger (1 to 2 inches long) and more elongated. Blackberries grow either on 4-foot-tall, erect canes or on trailing vines. Cane varieties thrive everywhere except in extremely cold or extremely warm regions, and vine types are limited to warmer climates. Boysenberries, loganberries, and dewberries are popular trailing varieties. Dewberries bear large, near-black berries; loganberries and boysenberries (*right*) are more red.

GOOSEBERRIES
■ One of the most popular bush fruits is the gooseberry (*opposite*). These tart, ¾-inch berries grow on thorny, 4-foot bushes in cold-winter regions. Berries are green, yellow, pink, or red. Because the gooseberry is an alternate host for white pine blister rust, its cultivation is banned in certain states.

BLUEBERRIES
■ There are several different types of blueberries, but only the high-bush blueberry (*Vaccinium corymbosum*) and rabbit-eye (*V. ashei*) are recommended for the home garden. Pinkish white flowers bloom in early spring, followed by blue fruit in June. Plant several varieties for cross-pollination.

ELDERBERRIES
■ Elderberries grow in the wild, but cultivated varieties of this hardy bush fruit also are available. Elderberries grow to 10 feet tall and bear purplish black berries in late summer. To ensure fruit production, plant two varieties, such as Adams and Johns.

GRAPES

Grape vines are perfect candidates for the small-lot garden. Use them on a trellis for privacy, or let them ramble over an arbor (*opposite*) for shade.

Plant two varieties to ensure cross-pollination. Most varieties are self-fertile but will produce larger clusters of fruit if interplanted. For an all-season crop, combine early-bearing varieties like Fredonia, Seedless, and Delaware with the mid- to late-season varieties, such as Niagara, Concord, Golden Muscat, Catawba, and Vinered.

HOW TO PLANT

■ Plant grapes in fall or in early spring as soon as the soil can be worked. Choose a sunny location that has rich, well-drained soil. Good air circulation also is necessary to prevent mildew, rot, and damage from spring frost. If possi-ble, run the vines in an east/west orientation to take full advantage of sunlight.

Before planting new stock, clip back roots to 8 or 12 inches long and vines to the second set of buds. Spread the roots out evenly in the planting hole. Space plants at least 8 feet apart. Side-dress with well-rotted manure or all-purpose fertilizer, and mulch with 2 to 4 inches of leaves or straw.

HOW TO PRUNE

■ At planting time, prune each vine to the best single cane, and prune that cane back to 2 or 3 buds. In following years, prune grapes in early spring while the vines are still dormant. If you want shade for a patio or screening for privacy, limit pruning to the removal of scraggly growth and old canes. Let a few new canes develop each year for a small harvest. Old canes produce only shade. A good grape arbor should provide plenty of ventilation around the canes to discourage mildew diseases.

If you grow grapes on a 2-wire trellis, such as in the drawing *below,* train the original cane to grow straight up a stake or string to the top wire. Cut the cane off just above the top wire to encourage arms. Train arms during the second growing season; all other shoots, suckers, and canes should be removed.

FERTILIZING

■ After spring planting, feed each vine with 4 ounces of 5-10-5 fertilizer, applying it no closer than 12 inches from the base of the trunk. In following years, feed as early in the spring as possible. Apply a pound and a half of fertilizer per mature vine.

Although most grapes are self-pollinating, you will get better results if you plant two varieties in your garden. Clusters of fruit will be larger. Harvest grapes when they're sweet and juicy.

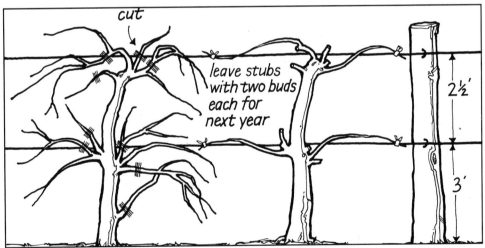

A good pruning method, called the four-arm "Kniffen system," is shown *above.* During the plant's second year, four arms are allowed to develop, two in each direction from the trunk, one set per wire.

Select four other canes, one from each of the original arms, and prune to two buds. These spurs will form new canes. The next spring, leave four canes and four spurs; remove all other wood.

STRAWBERRIES

Nothing beats the flavor of garden-ripe strawberries, freshly plucked from the backyard patch. Because they give luscious rewards without a lot of work, strawberries provide a great starting point for beginning fruit growers. Tuck single plants into a vegetable garden, or mass several together to make an ornamental and edible ground cover. Or, if your garden is limited to patio space, grow strawberries in a strawberry jar

(*opposite*). Ask a horticulturist at your local nursery about what varieties are suited for your region.

Plant sets in any sunny, well-drained garden location. To save money, you also can grow strawberries from seed. Sow seeds indoors six to eight weeks before outdoor planting. For a bumper crop the second year after planting, remove first-year runners and blossoms as soon as they appear.

TYPES OF STRAWBERRIES

■ **Everbearing.** Their name may imply continuous harvests, but everbearing strawberries actually produce two separate crops each year. Their first crop ripens in June, followed by a heavier second crop of smaller berries in early fall. Because they require a long growing season, everbearing varieties are not always recommended for northern regions. Popular varieties include Ogallala, Dunlap, Geneva, Ozark Beauty, and Superfection.

■ **June-bearing.** June-bearers produce fruit in early summer. Although plants offer a bigger summer yield than everbearing types do, they stop fruit production after the first harvest. In the June-bearing group, try Earliglow, Fairfax, Surecrop, or Sparkle.

■ **Day-neutral.** Newer day-neutral varieties produce berries all summer long. Unlike conventional strawberry plants, which bear only in the cool days of early June (or, in the case of everbearing, in June and again in the fall), day-neutral strawberries produce their flowers and fruit regardless of day length. That means you can serve up fresh strawberry shortcake in the winter, too, if you move your plants indoors and tend them carefully. Tristar, Tribute, and Brighton are three recommended day-neutral varieties.

■ **Alpine.** Unlike their cultivated cousins, alpine strawberries do not send out runners. Instead, they form compact mounds that are perfect for edgings around vegetable, flower, or herb gardens. Fruits are small and very sweet, much like the strawberries you find growing wild. Each plant will bloom for many years. Try Alexandria or Ruegen Improved for best results.

CARE AND MAINTENANCE

Strawberry plants will set fruit their first season, but they'll be more productive if you make them wait a year. For maximum results, plant strawberries in well-prepared soil and pinch off all blossoms the first season. That way, plants can store up berry-making power to make a jumbo harvest the following year.

SOIL PREPARATION

■ Strawberries require a well-drained, weed-free planting bed. If you're breaking ground for the first time, consider planting a vegetable crop in that space the first year. That way, the soil will be in better condition and rid of stubborn weeds by the second year. Before planting strawberries, spade in plenty of compost, and apply a complete fertilizer, such as 5-10-5.

GROWING METHODS

■ Proper planting depth should get top priority when you set out new strawberry transplants. Match the new soil line with the depth that the plant grew at the nursery. Make sure roots are completely underground, but avoid covering the crown. Mulch will help keep fruit clean, conserve moisture, and suppress weeds.

The technique you use for growing strawberries will depend on the size of berry and yield you want. Close, dense planting results in heavy yields of smaller berries, and open, well-spaced planting offers a lower yield but larger berries. The chief difference between each system is what you do with the runners, the baby plants that develop from the main plant.

■ Hill planting. For large berries and a neatly manicured strawberry bed, set plants 12 inches apart in rows spaced about 18 inches apart. Remove all run-

ners as they develop. This method results in healthy, strong central plants that bear maximum-size berries.

■ Matted row. For the least maintenance, use the matted-row planting method. Set transplants 18 to 24 inches apart, and after the first growing season, allow runners to root where they land. The result will be an informal mass instead of tidy rows. Remove first-year blossoms to strengthen plants. You'll get a bumper crop of smaller berries the following year.

REJUVENATING AN OLD BED

■ A well-cared-for strawberry patch can last up to five years. To renew a matted-row bed, cut plants back with a rotary mower set at a 4-inch cutting height. Feed with a 5-10-5 fertilizer and water. To prevent disease and insect problems, replace plants after five years.

Encourage runners (no more than six per mother plant) to form new plants every 9 inches. Pin down the runners with U-shaped pins or bury stems with soil. Remove unwanted runners.

1 Buy disease-free strawberry transplants from a reputable nursery. Spade soil to a depth of 8 to 10 inches, and mix in compost or manure to improve drainage.

2 Set plants at the same depth they grew at the nursery, with the crown planted just above the soil line. Spread the roots evenly over the soil mound.

3 Cover the roots with soil and gently firm into place. As you work, protect all unplanted strawberries by covering them with wet burlap or newspaper.

For large yields, use the matted-row planting method. Set the transplants 18 to 24 inches apart, and allow runners to root where they land. The result will be a solid mass instead of tidy rows.

To get jumbo-size berries, follow the hill planting method. Set plants 12 inches apart in rows spaced 18 inches apart. Pinch off all runners when they appear, to encourage a strong central plant.

Give strawberry plants a winter mulch after the first fall frost. In spring, loosen the mulch as plants turn green, but don't remove it completely until temperatures are dependably warm.

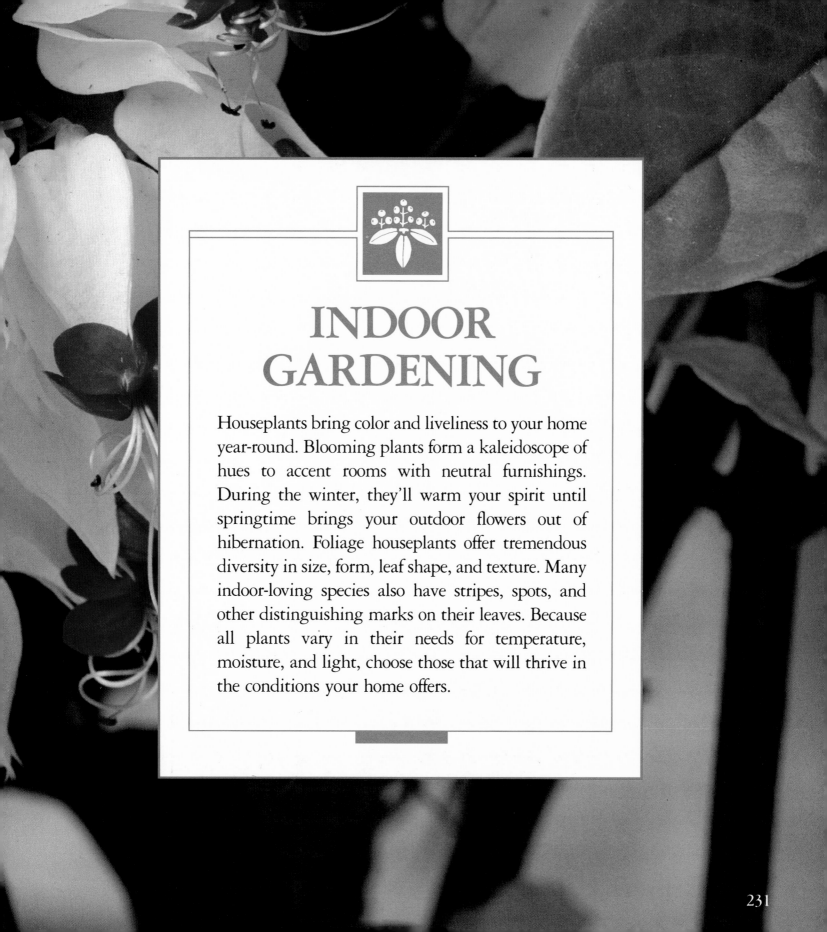

INDOOR GARDENING

Houseplants bring color and liveliness to your home year-round. Blooming plants form a kaleidoscope of hues to accent rooms with neutral furnishings. During the winter, they'll warm your spirit until springtime brings your outdoor flowers out of hibernation. Foliage houseplants offer tremendous diversity in size, form, leaf shape, and texture. Many indoor-loving species also have stripes, spots, and other distinguishing marks on their leaves. Because all plants vary in their needs for temperature, moisture, and light, choose those that will thrive in the conditions your home offers.

GARDENING INDOORS

Whether it's a full-fledged greenhouse with space for rows of colorful blooms and foliage, a brightly lighted windowsill, or just a dim corner that needs uplifting, there's a spot in your home that can benefit from the beauty and charm of indoor plants.

Existing conditions—especially the amount of light—may well be the deciding factor in what you grow. Unless you are growing plants under artificial lights, you will need to rely on light from windows, walls, or skylights, and select your plants accordingly.

LOW-LIGHT FAVORITES
■ Most indoor gardens are limited by poor lighting conditions, but fortunately a large number of plants will adapt to low light. These include ferns, Chinese evergreen (*Aglaonema modestum*), split-leaf philodendron (*Monstera deliciosa*), grape ivy (cissus), cast-iron plant (*Aspidistra elatior*), snake plant (*Sansevieria trifasciata*), pothos (epipremnum), and parlor palm (*Chamaedorea elegans*). The spathe flower (spathiphyllum) will grow in low light but needs bright light to produce flowers.

MEDIUM-LIGHT GROWERS
■ Medium or diffused light calls for spider plant (anthericum); dumb cane (dieffenbachia); dracaena; false aralia (dizygotheca); ficus, including rubber plant (*Ficus elastica*), fiddleleaf fig, and weeping fig (*F. benjamina*); prayer plant (*Maranta leuconeura*); peperomias, philodendrons, and pileas; Swedish ivy (plectranthus); piggyback plant (*Tolmiea menziesi*); wandering Jew (tradescantia or zebrina); syngonium; zebra plant (*Aphelandra squarrosa*); Norfolk Island pine (*Araucaria heterophylla*); schefflera (brassaia); and asparagus ferns.

Although most of the indoor flowering plants prefer full sun or very bright light, begonias, gloxinias, African violets (saintpaulia), some orchids, fuchsia, flame violets (episcia), and clivia will do well in an indirect light situation.

BRIGHT-LIGHT LOVERS
■ When the sun shines through windowpanes and directly hits the plants, you will need to select a high-intensity plant. This includes most flowering plants, cacti, succulents, and those with colorful leaves, such as croton and coleus. During the heat of summer, a southern exposure can be too intense, and plants may need a summer vacation in a spot with less intense light.

When strong light hits your indoor garden, choose from aloe, jade plant (*Crassula arborescens*), echeveria, velvet plant (gynura), English ivy (*Hedera helix*), kalanchoe, pittosporum, podocarpus, strawberry geranium (*Saxifraga stolonifera*), sedum, agave, bromeliads, ti plant (*Cordyline terminalis*), euphorbia, poinsettia, wax plant (hoya), scented geranium (pelargonium), Christmas cactus, and clerodendrum.

GALLERY OF HOUSEPLANTS

COLUMNEA
Columnea species

Graceful, arching stems make columnea particularly attractive for hanging baskets. Foliage, 1½ to 4 inches long, is usually shiny, bearing little resemblance to the foliage of its close relative, the African violet. Flowers, with a long, tubular shape, can appear singularly or in clusters. They come in bright shades of scarlet, orange, and yellow. These plants have a long flowering period, so their blooms can cheer up the home all winter long.
SOIL: Keep soil evenly moist.
LIGHT: Bright indirect, but no full sun
COMMENTS: Columnea will do well in any spot where African violets seem to thrive, although they do like it a little bit cooler than their cousins. Keep the humidity high by misting frequently. *Columnea crassifolia* has stems that first grow upright, and then trail.

CROWN-OF-THORNS
Euphorbia mili

This succulent plant does very well in the house, because it tolerates the dry conditions found in most homes during the winter months. The stems are thick and somewhat shrubby, and the entire stem is covered with thorns. Flowers, which actually are made of colored bracts around inconspicuous central blooms, come in shades of bright pink, yellow, orange, red, or coral. A mature plant has a rounded shape about 12 inches high. Foliage is round, thin, and light in color.
SOIL: Allow media to dry out between waterings. Apply more water when in growth or flower.
LIGHT: Full sun
COMMENTS: Grow crown-of-thorns in a media that is fast draining, porous, and has extra sharp sand or perlite added. Water sparingly in winter.

FERNS
Varied genera and species

Ferns, a Victorian favorite, have returned to popularity. The fronds are most graceful and there are a number of forms available.
SOIL: Keep soil evenly moist.
LIGHT: Indirect light, but no full sun
COMMENTS: Humidity is the key in growing ferns. Mist regularly, use a humidifier, or place them in the bathroom. Potting soil must be rich. Feed lightly only during periods of new growth and avoid touching new fronds, which may kill them. Avoid placing them in drafts.

Boston fern (*Nephrolepis exaltata*), with its lovely, curled fronds, is among the most popular ferns. The fronds of the bird's-nest fern (*Asplenium nidus*) are not divided. The staghorn fern (*Platycerium bifurcatum*) has large, antler-shape fronds that grow from a paperlike base. The delicate and airy maidenhair fern (*Adiantum pedatum*) has wiry stems and fan-shape fronds.

FICUS (weeping fig)
Ficus benjamina

This ornamental relative of the edible fig has small, waxy, pointed leaves that appear along the slightly drooping branches. Foliage measures about 5 inches long. Plants can become quite large—to 6 feet or more—and should be used only in large foyers, rooms, or other open spaces.

SOIL: Keep soil moist to the touch.

LIGHT: Bright, indirect light. Full sun will burn leaves, but too little sun will cause them to shed.

COMMENTS: Use a general potting soil that has extra sand or perlite added. Feed 3 to 4 times a year with an all-purpose fertilizer. If weeping fig starts to decline, move it to a spot with brighter light. New plants often lose their leaves when adapting to a new environment, but regain them if conditions are right. If possible, keep the humidity high.

HIBISCUS
Hibiscus rosa-sinensis

This shrubby cousin of the hollyhock and the rose-of-sharon grows 4 feet high and produces showy, 4- to 8-inch blooms in bright shades of red, pink, purple, orange, yellow, and white. The funnel-shaped flowers have a prominent pistil and may be single or double. They bloom mostly in summer or fall. When the plant is not in bloom, the dark green, glossy foliage is attractive.

SOIL: Keep evenly moist when in flower; keep dry at other times.

LIGHT: Full sun is necessary for hibiscus plants to flower.

COMMENTS: Hibiscus likes to be in a warm spot when it is growing and in flower, and in a cool area at other times. In spring, before new growth, prune back to half-size and repot if necessary. Keep humidity high. Use a standard potting soil and feed lightly only when in growth or flower. Pinch back tips to keep compact and bushy.

IVY
Hedera species

Trailing ivies can create gardens in windows or overhead areas in any room of the house. Ivy will also climb a pole or other support, or can be set to grow on a topiary form. English ivy (*H. helix*) has many variations in leaf size, shape, and color. Foliage can be 3-, 5-, or 7-lobed, dark green or variegated.

SOIL: Keep soil evenly moist.

LIGHT: Filtered, but not direct sun

COMMENTS: English ivy prefers a cool room and a high humidity. Regular misting keeps the humidity high and discourages red spider mites—a common problem with ivy. Use average potting soil and feed only in the spring and summer when the plant is growing.

Two other plants that are not true ivies are the German ivy (*Senecio mikanioides*) and the grape ivy (*Cissus rhombifolia*). They will thrive in lower light and in a warmer room. Grape ivy should receive little if any fertilizer.

235

GALLERY OF HOUSEPLANTS

KALANCHOE
Kalanchoe blossfeldiana

This succulent features thick, waxy leaves with smooth or scalloped reddish edges—each leaf growing about 2 inches long. Clusters of small red, orange, yellow, pink, or coral flowers are long-lasting. A popular gift plant, kalanchoe blooms in winter, when days are short. The mature plant reaches between 10 and 18 inches in height.

SOIL: Let soil dry out between waterings. Water slightly heavier when the plant is blooming.

LIGHT: Full sun

COMMENTS: Use a loose potting mixture with extra sharp sand or perlite added. Feed occasionally when in growth or flower. Kalanchoe prefers a cool room, especially at night. It is sometimes difficult to get a kalanchoe to rebloom, because they must not receive any stray light during the night. There are many named hybrids of this attractive, easy-to-grow, colorful plant.

ORCHID
Mixed genera and species

Although most orchids do best in the environment of the greenhouse, there are some that will do very well in the house. The moth orchid (phalaenopsis), with flowers of white, pink, or yellow; the lady slipper (paphiopedilum or cypripedium), with solid or spotted flowers in many colors; or the cymbidiums, with racemes of white, yellow, or green flowers, will do the best indoors. They still do prefer high humidity of a greenhouse environment.

SOIL: Potting medium should be kept evenly moist at all times.

LIGHT: Cymbidiums like the most light or full sun; the others like a very bright, indirect light.

COMMENTS: Grow orchids in a medium of osmunda or fir bark made especially for orchids. A small amount of peat moss can be added to help retain the water. Grow on pebble trays to keep humidity high. Small orchids thrive in terrariums.

PEPEROMIA
Peperomia species

Varied foliage is the distinguishing characteristic of this plant. The thick, semi-succulent leaves may be smooth, shiny green, two-toned, corrugated, or deeply ridged, with red, pink, or green stems which can be trailing or upright. Flowers are long, dense, thick stalks.

SOIL: Allow soil to dry between waterings. Water less in winter.

LIGHT: Bright light, but not direct sun. Filter intense light.

COMMENTS: Use an average potting soil with extra sand or perlite added, and feed only during growth periods.

Try Emerald-ripple (*P. caperata*), with deeply ridged and quilted dark green and brown leaves; the ivy peperomia (*P. griseoargentea*) that has a silver sheen on the leaves; the watermelon peperomia (*P. argyreia*), with green and white striped leaves; or blunt-leaved (*P. obtusifolia*), which climbs when young and trails at maturity.

PILEA
Pilea species

Pileas are small plants that have trailing stems and plain or fancy leaves. These leaves can be deeply textured or brightly colored.

SOIL: Keep evenly moist.

LIGHT: Bright, indirect or filtered sun

COMMENTS: Potting soil should be rich, so add extra peat moss. Feed lightly every two months, and take measures to keep humidity high. Pinch out growing tips if they become too leggy.

One of the best known pileas is the aluminum plant (*P. cadierei*), which has thin, quilted leaves with silver-colored streaks over blue-green foliage. Moon Valley has deeply veined, quilted leaves of apple green, textured brown foliage, and clusters of tiny pink flowers. Silver Tree is dark brown and silver, with veined and quilted leaves. The artillery plant (*P. microphylla*) has tiny leaves and is a good plant for a hanging basket.

TRADESCANTIA (wandering Jew)
Tradescantia species

This easy-to-grow houseplant has a flat growing or trailing habit that makes an excellent choice for hanging baskets. The fast growing stems are succulent, with swollen joints from where leaves of green, striped yellow or striped purple and green grow. Oval or pointed leaves are 2 to 2½ inches long. Small, white flowers are barely noticeable.

SOIL: Allow soil surface to almost dry out before rewatering.

LIGHT: Full sun to indirect light

COMMENTS: Use an all-purpose soil mix. Wandering Jew does very well in normal household humidity, but does best when kept slightly cool. In the summer, move it outdoors for containers, window boxes, and ground covers. It roots easily and can be increased quite readily.

VIOLET, AFRICAN
Saintpaulia species

It is from Africa, but this plant really is not a violet. Nevertheless, African violets are among the most popular of houseplants. They bloom year-round, with single or double flowers of pink, purple, blue, violet, rose, or white. Some flowers are bicolored; many are ruffled, crimped, wavy, or frilled. The leaves are velvety green, some with a metallic cast.

SOIL: Water as soon as the soil surface becomes dry; avoid touching the leaves with water.

LIGHT: Bright, indirect light

COMMENTS: African violets like high humidity, so grow on pebble trays. Potting soil should be extra rich, yet well drained. Fertilizer can be used all year. They like normal indoor temperatures and must be kept from drafts. Leaves that touch the rim of a porous clay pot (where soluble salts accumulate) often rot and fall off. To avoid the problem, transplant to a plastic pot.

GARDENING UNDER LIGHTS

Try fooling Mother Nature by creating a perfect, natural habitat for your houseplants under lights. The intensity of the light, day length, temperature, water, humidity, pest control, and air movement are in your hands.

Artificial light allows you to grow plants anywhere in the house. You can locate light gardens in the living room, office, attic, kitchen, spare room, basement, and even a closet.

WHICH ARTIFICIAL LIGHT?
■ To grow plants under lights, you need to understand a little bit about the science of artificial light. All white light is composed of the colors of a rainbow: red, orange, yellow, green, blue, indigo, and violet. Reading light is mostly green and yellow—two colors not used by plants. Plants need the cool blue and violet tones to grow foliage, and the warm red and orange to produce flowers. Therefore, use cool light only on foliage plants and both cool and warm lights on flowering plants.

Fluorescent grow lights are available that are designed especially for plants. Regular fluorescent lights can be used for foliage plants; wider-spectrum lights should be used for flowering plants. You can also combine regular cool and warm white tubes in equal numbers.

An incandescent bulb gives off a good amount of red light, but since it also gives off a lot of heat, it's not recommended for use in a light garden.

HOW MUCH LIGHT?
■ The next step is to determine the amount of light or intensity. Flowering plants need a higher intensity, but you will have to experiment with each type and situation. Too much intensity pro-

duces compact growth; too little will produce growth that is leggy and flowers poorly. To increase intensity, use longer tubes or more of them, place them closer together, use white reflectors, move the plants closer to the tubes or the center of the tubes, or burn the lights longer. Do the opposite to decrease intensity.

HOW LONG IS A DAY?
■ Day length is very important, and in some cases, determines when a plant flowers. To get plants to perform when

you want them to, supplement or substitute natural lighting conditions with artificial lights. The Christmas cactus and the kalanchoe need short days to bloom. For plants that need long days, burn lights over those that flower for 16 hours a day and those that produce foliage only for 12 hours. Turn lights on and off at the same time every day to provide consistent conditions. This can best be controlled with a timer. Remember that plants on the top shelf of a multi-tiered light box will be warmer, and dry out faster, than the others.

PLANT PROPAGATION

You can enlarge your houseplant collection inexpensively by propagating the plants you already have. Depending on the plant, choose from among the following methods: seeds, root divisions, runners and offsets, cuttings (leaf and stem), and air layering. All of these methods, except seeding, are asexual or vegetative forms of reproduction.

Use pots, flats, jars, or terrariums to start new plants. Choose a container that is deep enough for root development and will provide a way to enclose the plant to keep humidity high.

Forsyth potting is a growing technique that involves placing a smaller flowerpot inside a larger one, and filling the space between the pots with sand or sphagnum peat moss. The filler is kept moist so the rooting medium will not dry out.

A GOOD MEDIUM MIX

■ A mixture of half coarse sand and half peat moss is a good choice for rooting medium. Perlite or vermiculite can substitute for sand. Peat moss will retain moisture; the others provide aeration.

CUTTINGS

■ Taking a cutting from a stem or leaf is one of the most common methods of propagating houseplants. Use stem cuttings to increase plants such as coleus, geranium, begonia, and ivy. Cut a stem just under a leaf node and carefully remove lower leaves. Remove any flowers and flower buds. Plant the stem in a container filled with propagating medium, cover with a plastic bag, and place in bright light (not full sun) until it's rooted (about 3 to 4 weeks).

Propagate African violets, begonias, gloxinias, and others with leaf cuttings. Take a leaf with a small section of stem and lay it on the medium, right side up, with stem inserted in medium. Cut the veins so new roots will form. For snake plants, cut a leaf into 2-inch sections and root each. Philodendrons, pothos, and

With root division, you split one plant into two or more parts. Remove the plant from the pot, wash off medium if necessary, and gently pull the roots apart. Repot each section in fresh medium.

wax plants are propagated from stem pieces that contain a leaf bud. Make new plants from dieffenbachias and dracaenas by laying cut-up cane pieces horizontally just under medium surface.

AIR LAYERING
■ Large, woody stemmed houseplants should be air layered by cutting partway through the stem and holding the cut open with a wedge. Wrap a ball of moist sphagnum peat moss around the cut and enclose it with plastic.

STARTING WITH SEEDS
■ Many plants, including coleus, Christmas cherry, gloxinia, and cineraria, can be grown from seed. Sow seeds in a fine medium; cover to same depth as their thickness. Then cover with plastic and germinate in good light, not full sun.

Stem or leaf cuttings will root more quickly if you dip the end of the cutting in a root-inducing hormone or paint hormone powder on the cutting.

Dieffenbachias can be propagated in one of two ways. Either take a stem cutting and root it in water, or cut a section of the cane and root it in medium.

Leaf cuttings can be rooted in a container of water. Transplant into potting medium as soon as roots form, because the transition from water to medium with mature roots is difficult.

Plants such as spider plants and strawberry begonias produce plantlets. These can be rooted by firming them into a small pot of medium. They can be removed from the parent before rooting.

New roots will form in the peat moss ball created when air layering woody stemmed plants. Once roots are well formed, you can cut the stem just below the root ball and plant the rooted cutting.

241

CARE AND MAINTENANCE

Growing houseplants successfully requires duplicating the plants' natural environment as closely as possible. This may include manipulating light, temperature, water, humidity, and fertility, and controlling pests.

WATERING

■ Watering is probably the most confusing aspect of indoor gardening, and the one that contributes most to plant performance or decline. Plants can suffer from either too much or too little water. Don't plan to water on a regular routine, because variables such as temperature or humidity can change from day to day. Two plants of the same type may not need identical watering, because the container size may be different. You must regularly feel the planting media to determine how often to water your plants.

Those plants that like to be drier should be watered heavily and not watered again until the top half inch feels dry. Those that like moderate watering should be watered when the soil surface becomes dry. The plants that like to be constantly moist should be kept damp but not soggy. Unless you are growing under lights, plants will need less water during winter's short days.

Always water enough to completely saturate the media, which happens when water flows out from the bottom of the pot. If your pot has a drainage saucer, be sure to empty it so roots do not sit in water and possibly rot.

Bottom or top watering? There are advantages to both methods. Bottom watering ensures that the media becomes completely soaked. Top watering flushes out salt buildup, which can be harmful to plants.

FEEDING

■ Plants, like their caretakers, will not do well without food. Unlike people, however, plants are not constant in their nutritional needs. When a plant is in a stage of active growth and flowering, feed it often but lightly. When a plant isn't growing or flowering—such as during the shorter days of winter—it should not be fed as frequently. A soluble fertilizer such as 20-20-20 works best, applied at one-fourth the amount that is recommended on the container label, four times as often.

Be careful not to overfeed. You'll produce a lush, soft growth, but also get a buildup of soluble salts that can damage roots or possibly kill plants. If accidental overfeeding occurs, flush media with water until runoff is colorless, indicating that all the salts have been leached away.

TEMPERATURE

■ Most indoor plants are tropical, preferring a household temperature of 70 degrees F. during the day and 60 degrees at night. If you want to grow plants that like cool conditions, the temperature should range between 60 and 70 degrees in the day, with a drop at night. Many plants that go dormant in winter prefer cooler temperatures. Don't let the plants freeze, and keep them protected from hot radiators and cold drafts from doors and windows.

NEW ARRIVALS

■ New plants need time to acclimatize to their new surroundings. Because light levels and humidity may be less at home than in the greenhouse, you can expect some leaves to drop. New leaves should replace the old. Keep humidity high during the transition period.

When it's time to repot, start with a new or clean pot and place a crockery chip over the drainage hole. Select a pot slightly larger than the first.

In one hand, hold the plant to be repotted; with the other hand, remove the pot. If necessary, rap the pot lightly on the edge of the bench to loosen the soil.

Hold the plant in the new pot at the right level. Fill in beneath the plant and around the roots with media. Water immediately to eliminate air pockets.

When repotting pot-bound plants, use a knife to loosen the outer part of the root ball. This is necessary to encourage new root growth and ensure continued plant vigor.

Handling cacti when they need to be transplanted can be a painful task. To save your hands, make a collar out of newspaper and use it to hold the plant.

Most plants should be watered immediately after transplanting. Cacti and other succulents, however, should sit dry for a few days to prevent rot.

CARE AND MAINTENANCE

Don't underestimate the value of the right amount of light for plants. Although a plant may not show the effect of too little light right away, in time it will deteriorate.

Plants are often classified as needing low, medium, or high light. As a guide, figure low light to be that from a north window, medium from an east or west window, and high from a south window. Another way to judge this is by the shadow cast by the plant. If it is barely discernible, the light is low; when the shadow is present but indistinct, light is medium; when the shadow is sharp, the light is bright. Choose plant types according to the light conditions you can give them. To keep a plant growing optimally, it may be necessary to rotate the plant every few weeks to prevent uneven growth.

It is also possible to give too much light to a plant, resulting in compacted growth and burned foliage. If this happens, move the plant away from the window to a new lower-light area, or put a sheer curtain on the window.

If you are going to be away from home for an extended period, there are several ways you can make sure your plants survive. If you can't get a "plant sitter," you can water with a wick running to each plant that draws from a supply of water, or you can enclose your plants in plastic bags. This will hold in the moisture and prolong the time between the waterings. Keep the plant out of a sunny window to prevent damage from high temperature. If you are moving, remember that many moving vans aren't heated or cooled, so plants can freeze or overheat.

Most plants, with the exception of cacti and succulents, like high humidity. Misting is a way to raise humidity, but you'll need to do it several times a day to be effective.

As flowers fade, keep them picked off to keep the plant's strength in growth and flower production and not in the production of seed. Prune any branches that become long or misshapen.

Another way to raise humidity around plants is to group them together on a gravel tray. Put enough gravel in the tray so plant roots will not sit in water.

Often, heat or dry conditions can cause plant foliage tips to turn brown and dry out. If this occurs, use scissors to cut off the browned tips at an angle.

Fronds of Boston ferns can turn brown. If this occurs, use scissors to cut out the frond at the base. Yellow or brown foliage on other plants also should be removed.

Large, smooth-leaved plants are frequently collectors of dust. In normal housekeeping chores, wash or wipe away dust to keep the plant attractive, and to keep it photosynthesizing at its best.

Hairy-leaved plants, such as the African violet also collect dust. Because moistening the leaves will cause unsightly spots, remove dust with a small paintbrush or by blowing it away.

If you have a pest problem, you will want to contain the pesticide, for both effectiveness and safety. Plastic around the plant will accomplish both. Remove the plastic after several days.

INSECTS AND DISEASES

INSECT OR DISEASE	DESCRIPTION AND TROUBLE SIGNS	CONTROLS
Aphids	Also called common plant lice, these insects are up to 1/8 inch long and can be green, red, black, or brown. They occur mostly on new growing tips and undersides of leaves. By sucking the plant juices, they cause the foliage to yellow and die. They also secrete a "honeydew."	If infestation is not too bad, wash it away in a strong stream of water. If that doesn't work, one or more sprays or dips of insecticide will be needed.
Brown leaf tips	Leaf edges turn crispy and brown, almost as if burned. New growth also quickly becomes brown and loses strength. This can be caused by too high heat, too low humidity, plants becoming too dry between waterings, drafts, or too much fertilizing.	Isolate the problem and correct it. Lower the temperature, raise the humidity, water more evenly, and carefully follow fertilizer directions.
Bud drop	Sometimes flower buds will form, but will drop off before flowering. The causes of this can be high temperatures, low humidity, drafts, uneven or insufficient watering, too much fertilizer, or shock from being moved too often while in the bud stage.	Isolate the problem and correct it. Avoid high temperatures, drafts, or too dry soil; keep humidity up.
Failure of plant to bloom	In this case, plants which should produce blooms do not. The reasons for this can be insufficient light or too much nitrogen fertilizer. Also, some blooming houseplants are dependent on day length, and must either be shaded or receive supplemental light to produce flowers.	Give bright light, lower fertilizer amounts, keep humidity high, and keep moisture even. Check to see if plants are sensitive to day length.
Mealybug	Mealybugs have soft, 1/4-inch-long bodies and a coating of white, powdery wax. They look like cotton balls clustered under leaves, in stem crotches, and on top of shaded leaves. They suck out plant juices and can kill plants.	Control by wetting each bug with rubbing alcohol, applied with a cotton swab. For severe infestations, spray or dip, using insecticide.

INSECT OR DISEASE	DESCRIPTION AND TROUBLE SIGNS	CONTROLS
Scale	Scales are oval or round ⅛-inch-long insects with a shell-like covering. Colors are generally white, gray, brown, or black. Scales deposit a sticky, shiny honeydew on leaves. They suck plant juices and can cause plant death.	Small numbers of scales can be easily removed with soapsuds. Where large numbers are present, use an approved insecticide as a spray or dip.
Spider mite	Spider mites are so tiny they can barely be seen, but you will notice yellow spots on the upper side of the leaves, an overall dull red look to the foliage, and fine webbing (where colonies are large).	Keep plants properly watered and keep humidity high. A dip in plain water on a regular basis will prevent spread. Use a miticide if necessary.
White fly	These white insects fly off the plants when stirred and can look like a white cloud. They suck plant juices, turning foliage yellow. If untreated, white flies will eventually kill the plant.	Several applications of an insecticide will probably be necessary. Wash your hands after handling infested plants to prevent spread of invisible eggs.
Wilt	Wilt—which can lead to a quick plant death—can be caused by too little water or a related condition, such as poor soil, high temperature, or low humidity. Wilt can also be caused by the opposite conditions, including too much water or a waterlogged or poorly drained soil.	Provide a lower temperature, water more often, raise the humidity, or check the root ball to see if the plant needs repotting.
Yellowing foliage	Foliage that turns yellow and falls off indicates many different things: too much or too little light; high temperature; overwatering or poor drainage; too much or too little fertilizer; or polluted air. A certain amount of yellowing foliage and leaf drop is normal and should be expected.	Check growing conditions to see if any could be causing the problem. Make sure the plant is not too hot, wet, or dry; has the right amount of light; and has enough fresh air.

CONSIDER YOUR CLIMATE

The climatic conditions in your area are a mixture of different weather patterns: sun, snow, rain, wind, and humidity. A good gardener is aware of all of the variations in temperature and conditions in his or her own garden, from how much rainfall it receives each year to the high and low temperatures of a typical growing season.

The zone map at *right* gives an approximate range of minimum temperatures across the country. Most plants are rated by these zones for conditions where they grow best.

However, zone boundary lines are not absolute. You can obtain the general information for your area from your state agricultural school or your county extension agent.

Be sure to study the microclimates that characterize your own plot of ground. Land on the south side of your house is bound to be warmer than a constantly shaded area exposed to cold, northwest winds. Being aware of the variations in your garden will help you choose the best plant for the prevailing conditions and avoid disappointment.

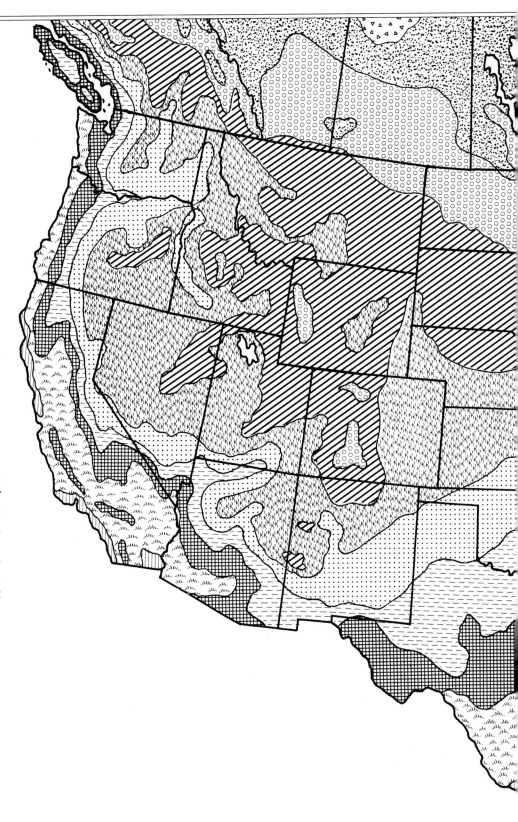

248

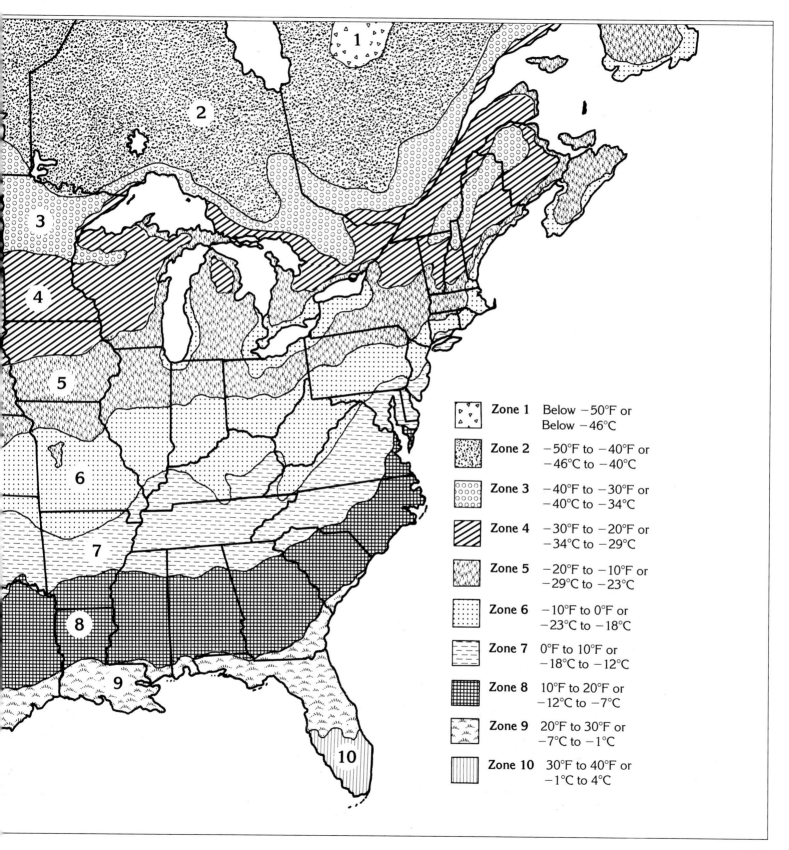

	Zone 1	Below −50°F or Below −46°C
	Zone 2	−50°F to −40°F or −46°C to −40°C
	Zone 3	−40°F to −30°F or −40°C to −34°C
	Zone 4	−30°F to −20°F or −34°C to −29°C
	Zone 5	−20°F to −10°F or −29°C to −23°C
	Zone 6	−10°F to 0°F or −23°C to −18°C
	Zone 7	0°F to 10°F or −18°C to −12°C
	Zone 8	10°F to 20°F or −12°C to −7°C
	Zone 9	20°F to 30°F or −7°C to −1°C
	Zone 10	30°F to 40°F or −1°C to 4°C

CREDITS

STEP-BY-STEP SUCCESSFUL GARDENING

The following credits, listed in order of their appearance in the book, are for the field editors, garden designers, landscape architects, and photographers whose work appears in this book. We extend our appreciation to all of them for their creative talents. *Note: Photographers' names appear in italics.*

Special thanks to field editor Bonnie Maharam and photographers *Bill Maris* and *Julie Semel*, who contributed to pages 34–35, 46–47, 58–59, 64–65, 78–81, 84–85, 92–93, 108–109, 116–117, 124–131, 148–153, 156–159, 178–179, 182–183, 188–189, 196–199, 216–221, and 230–231.

Thanks to photographer *Peter Krumhardt* for his work on pages 16–17, 66–67, 82–83, 96–97, 110–111, 132–133, 134–135, 140–141, 144–147, 164–165, 174–175, 192–193, 202–203, and 208–209.

Photographs by *Hopkins Associates* appear on pages 44–45, 68–69, 200–201, and 238–239.

Photographs by *Wm. Hopkins* appear on pages 4–15, 60–61, 94–95, and 170–171.

Pages 18–19
Cathy Howard
Garden design:
Faith Mackaness
Karlis Grants
Pages 20–21
Estelle Bond Guralnick
Garden design:
Anne Davidson
Maris/Semel
Pages 22–23
Mary Anne Thomson
Maris/Semel
Peter Krumhardt
Pages 24–27
Illustrations courtesy of
O.M. Scott & Sons
Pages 28–29
Bonnie Maharam
Maris/Semel
Hopkins Associates
Pages 30–31
Bonnie Maharam
Sharon Haven
Maris/Semel
Kim Brun
Pages 32–33
Barbara Cathcart
Bonnie Maharam
De Gennaro Studios
Fred Lyon
Maris/Semel
Pages 36–37
De Gennaro Studios
Pages 38–39
Bonnie Maharam
Sharon Haven

Helen Heitkamp
Maris/Semel
Kim Brun
Ernest Braun
Pages 40–41
Bonnie Maharam
Maris/Semel
Hopkins Associates
Bill Helms
Pages 42–43
Bonnie Maharam
Bill Helms
Maris/Semel
Pages 48–49
Bonnie Maharam
Pauline Graves
Wm. Hopkins
Hopkins Associates
Maris/Semel
De Gennaro Studios
Pages 50–51
Bonnie Maharam
Hopkins Associates
Peter Krumhardt
Maris/Semel
Pages 52–53
Peter Krumhardt
Hopkins Associates
Page 54–55
Bonnie Maharam
Dorothy Campbell
Hopkins Associates
Wm. Hopkins
De Gennaro Studios
Guy Burgess
Page 56–57
Peter Krumhardt
Wm. Hopkins
Hopkins Associates
Pages 62–63
Bonnie Maharam
Maris/Semel

Peter Krumhardt
Hopkins Associates
Pages 70–71
Bonnie Maharam
Helen Heitkamp
Maris/Semel
Ernest Braun
Pages 72–77
Bonnie Maharam
Maris/Semel
Peter Krumhardt
Pages 88–89
Sharon Haven
Barbara Cathcart
Kim Brun
Tim Street-Porter
Pages 90–91
Sharon Haven
Bonnie Maharam
Pauline Graves
Kim Brun
Maris/Semel
De Gennaro Studios
Pages 98–99
Pauline Graves
De Gennaro Studios
Pages 100–101
George Ceolla
Pages 102–103
Bonnie Maharam
Maris/Semel
George Ceolla
Pages 104–105
Bonnie Maharam
Maris/Semel
George Ceolla
Pages 106–107
George Ceolla
De Gennaro Studios
Pages 112–113
Mary Anne Thomson
Bonnie Maharam

Hopkins Associates
Maris/Semel
Pages 114–115
 Bonnie Maharam
 Pat Carpenter
 Maris/Semel
 Hopkins Associates
Pages 118–119
 Paintings: Parker Heath
Pages 120–121
 Bonnie Maharam
 Pauline Graves
 Barbara Cathcart
 Maris/Semel
 De Gennaro Studios
 Ernest Braun
Pages 122–123
 Bonnie Maharam
 Maris/Semel
 Hopkins Associates
Pages 130–131
 Garden design:
 Panfield Nursery
Pages 132–133
 Bonnie Maharam
 Peter Krumhardt
 Maris/Semel
Pages 136–137
 Pauline Graves
 Bonnie Maharam
 De Gennaro Studios
 Maris/Semel
Pages 138–139
 Bonnie Maharam
 Bill Helms
 Maris/Semel
Pages 142–143
 Bonnie Maharam
 Maris/Semel
 Peter Krumhardt
Pages 154–155
 Bonnie Maharam

Maris/Semel
Hopkins Associates
Pages 160–163
 Bonnie Maharam
 Peter Krumhardt
 Maris/Semel
Pages 166–167
 Barbara Cathcart
 Mary Anne Thomson
 Ernest Braun
 Hopkins Associates
Pages 168–169
 Estelle Bond Guralnick
 Garden design:
 Peter and Patty Abbott
 Ewing Walker
 Ozzie Sweet
Pages 172–173
 Bonnie Maharam
 Garden design:
 Dick Raymond/
 Garden Way
 Donald Ross
 Ozzie Sweet
 Bill Helms
Pages 174–175
 Garden design:
 Don Peschke
Pages 176–177
 Cathy Howard
 Garden design:
 Peter Chan
 Karlis Grants
Pages 180–181
 Cathy Howard
 Mary Anne Thomson
 Peter Krumhardt
 Ozzie Sweet
 Hopkins Associates
 Karlis Grants
Pages 186–187
 Estelle Guralnick

Garden design: Jan Hall
Maureen Ruettgers
Maris/Semel
Pages 190–191
 Estelle Guralnick
 Garden design:
 Maureen Ruettgers
 Margy Mirick
 Maris/Semel
Pages 194–195
 Bonnie Maharam
 Sharon Haven
 Garden design:
 Alice Menard
 Maris/Semel
 Rick Taylor
 Kim Brun
Pages 204–205
 Bonnie Maharam
 Maris/Semel
 Hopkins Associates
Pages 210–211
 Bonnie Maharam
 Helen Heitkamp
 Maris/Semel
 Ernest Braun
Pages 212–213
 Bonnie Maharam
 Maris/Semel
 Ernest Braun
 Peter Krumhardt
Pages 214–215
 Bonnie Maharam
 Maris/Semel
 Peter Krumhardt
Pages 216–217
 Illustrations: Susan Maher
Pages 222–223
 Dorothy Campbell
 Bonnie Maharam
 De Gennaro Studios
 Maris/Semel

Pages 224–225
 Bonnie Maharam
 Garden design:
 Gay Gillespie
 Maris/Semel
 Bill Helms
Pages 226–227
 Pauline Graves
 Hopkins Associates
 De Gennaro Studios
Pages 228–229
 Bonnie Maharam
 Maris/Semel
 Ross Chapple
Pages 232–233
 Bonnie Maharam
 Bill Helms
Pages 234–235
 Hopkins Associates
 Jessie Walker
Pages 236–237
 Bonnie Maharam
 Maris/Semel
 Jessie Walker
 Guy Burgess
Pages 240–241
 Bonnie Maharam
 Sharon Haven
 Maris/Semel
 Kim Brun
Pages 242–245
 Jessie Walker
 Bonnie Maharam
 Hedrich-Blessing
 Maris/Semel
Pages 248–249
 Map courtesy of
 United States
 Department of
 Agriculture

INDEX

A

Aconite, winter, 149
Aegopodium, 32
African violet, 237, 245
Air layering, 241
Ajuga, 30, 32
Allium, 148
Almond, flowering, 55
Alpine strawberries, 226
American Rose Society, 198
Andromeda, 48
Anemone, 148
Animals
  attracting, trees for, 70
  protecting bulbs, 147, 153
Annuals, 87–109
  care and maintenance, 108–109
  in containers, 91, 100 102, 104, 106
  herbs, 188, 189
  lights, growing under, 94
  seedlings, 92, 95, 96–97
  from transplants, 98–99
  vines, 40, 42
Aphids, 184, 206, 246
Apples, 212
Apple trees, 210
  crab apple, 72
Arborvitae, 63
Armyworms, 26
Asarabacca, 133
Astilbe, 120
Azaleas, 50

B

Balled-and-burlapped
  (B&B) plants
  shrubs, 58, 59
  trees, 78–79

Barberries, 50
Bare-root plants
  roses, 200, 201
  shrubs, 58–59
  trees, 78
Bark, damaged, 85
Basil, sweet, 188
Baskets, hanging, 102–103
Beans and peas, 182
Bearded irises, 122, 124
Bedding plants, 98–99
Beetles, 184
  Japanese, 206
Begonias, tuberous, 160–163
Berries
  cane and bush, 220–223
  strawberries, 226–229
Biennials, 136–139
  parsley, 188
Billbugs, 26
Birch, 72
Birds, protecting fruit
  from, 219, 223
Bishop's weed, 32
Blackberries, 220
Black-eyed susan, 128
Black-eyed susan vine, 40
Black spot, 206
Bloodroot, 132
Blueberries, 220, 222, 223
Borage, 188
Borders. *See* Perennials
Borers, 184
Bougainvillea, 39
Boxwood, 50
Boysenberries, 220
Braiding bulb foliage, 152
Broccoli, harvesting, 183
Broom, Scotch, 51
Brown leaf tips, 245, 246
Buckwheat, 172
Bud drop, 246
Bugleweed (ajuga), 30, 32

Bulbs, 141–163
  care and maintenance, 152–153
  forcing, 154–155
  lilies, hardy 156–157
  summer-blooming, 158–163
  care and maintenance, 162–163
Burning bush, 52
Bush fruits, 220–221
  care and maintenance, 222, 223
Buttercup, 32

C

Cacti, transplanting, 243
Caladiums, 158–161
Calla lilies, 160
Camellias, 51
Candytuft, 120
Cane fruits, 220
  care and maintenance, 222, 223
Canker, 206
Canna lilies, 158
  rhizomes, 163
Canterbury-bells, 136, 138
Carpet bugle (ajuga), 30, 32
Caterpillars, 26, 184
  leaf rollers, 206
Cauliflower, blanching, 183
Ceanothus, 51
Celery plants, 180
Cherries, 212
Cherry trees, 68
  flowering, 76
  weeping, 80
Chickweed, mouse-ear, 24
Chinch bugs, 26
Chinese junipers, 71

Chinese peonies, 125
Chionodoxa, 148
Chrysanthemum, 120
Clematis, 38, 40, 43
Climatic zones, 248–249
Climbers (roses), 194, 198
  pruning, 203
Cold frames, 129, 180–181
Coleus, rooting, 109
Colonial garden, 169
Color categories, roses, 198
Columbine, 132
Columnea, 234
Containerized plants
  roses, 200
  shrubs, 58, 59
  trees, 78, 214
Container plants
  annuals, 91, 100–107
  fruit trees, 210, 214
  strawberry jars, 104, 227
Cool-season annuals, 96
Cool-season crops, 170
  bolting by, 183
Cool-season grasses, 18
Coreopsis, 121
Corms, gladiolus, 163
Couch grass, 25
Cowslip, 132
Crab apple, 72
Crabgrass, common, 24
Cranberry, highbush, 52
Crape myrtle, 75
Creeping myrtle, 33
Crickets, mole, 27
Crocus, 149
Cross pollination, 212
Crown-of-thorns, 234
Cup-and-saucer vine, 41
Currants, 222
Cuttings, propagating with
  annuals, 109
  houseplants, 240–241
Cutworms, 26, 182, 184

D

Daffodils, 149, 153
Dahlias, 160, 162, 163
Daisy, English, 136, 138
Dandelion, 24
Daylilies, 121, 126
Day-neutral strawberries, 226
Deadheading
  annuals, 108
  perennials, 128
Dead nettle, 32
Delphinium, 121
Demonstration garden, 167
Dieffenbachias, 241
Dill, 189
Disbudding, 162, 204
Diseases
  houseplants, 246, 247
  roses, 206–207
  vegetables, 185
Dividing
  bulbs, 153, 162
  ground covers, 35
  houseplants, 240
  perennials, 124–129
Dock, curly, 24
Dog-tooth violet, 135
Dogwoods, 52, 70, 72
Dormant oil spray, 64, 84
Double cropping, 172
Drip irrigation, 10, 166
Drying herbs, 190
Dust, removing, 245
Dutchman's-breeches, 133
Dutchman's-pipe, 41
Dwarf fruit trees, 210, 211, 214

E

Elderberries, 220, 222
English daisy, 136, 138
English ivy, 235
Epimedium, 33
Eranthis, 149
Espalier pruning, 216–217
Euonymus
  winged, 52
  winter creeper, 33
Everbearing strawberries, 226
Evergreen shrubs, 46, 48, 51, 57
  for privacy hedges, 63
  pruning, 61
  winter protection of, 65
Evergreen trees, 75, 76
  pruning, 80
  for screening, 71
  winter protection for, 84

F

Fall color, leaves for 49, 70
Feeding. See Fertilizer
Ferns, 33, 234
  Boston, brown ends, 245
Fertilizer
  annuals, 108
  application of, 13
  bulbs, 152
  components of, 12
  grapes, 224
  houseplants, 242
  lawns, 22
  roses, 204
  shrubs, 64
  trees, 84
Fig (ficus)
  weeping, 235
  winter protection, 219
Floribunda, 196
Flower gardens, plants for.
  See Annuals; Bulbs;
    Perennials; Roses
Flowering almond, 55

Flowering cherries, 76
Fluorescent lights
  for annuals, 94
  for houseplants, 238
Fly, white, 247
Foliage. See Leaves
Forcing bulbs, 154–155
Formal vs. informal bulb
  gardens, 146
Forsythia, 53, 62, 65
  potting, 240
Foxglove, 136, 138
Fritillaria, 150
Fruits and berries 208–209
  cane and bush, 220–221
    care and maintenance, 222, 223
  grapes and grapevines, 210–211, 224–225
  strawberries, 225–227
    care and maintenance, 228–229
  trees, 210–211
    care and maintenace, 218–219
    planting, 214
    pruning, 215–217
    selecting, 212
Fungus diseases, 185, 206, 207
Funkia, 122

G

Galanthus, 150
Ginger, wild, 133
Ginkgo, 73
Gladiolus, 158
  corms, 163
Glory-of-the-snow, 148
Golden-chain tree, 73
Gooseberries, 220, 221, 222
Goutweed, 32

Grandiflora, 196
Grapes and grapevines, 210–211, 224–225
Grass. See also Lawns
  cool-season and warm-season, 18
  as cover crops, 172
  ornamental, 33
Grecian windflower, 148
Ground covers, 29–35
  choosing and using, 34
  dividing and planting, 35
Grubs, white, 26

H

Hanging baskets, 102–103
Hawthorn, 73
Heading back, 60–61
Heaths and heathers, 31
Hedges, 62–63
  pruning, 64
  rose, 194
Hepatica, 133
Herbs, 186–191
  care and maintenance, 190
Hibiscus, 48, 235
Highbush cranberry, 52
Hill planting, 228–229
Holly, 53
Hollyhocks, 128, 136
Honesty, 139
Honeysuckle, 38, 53
  hedge, 63
Hosta, 122
Houseplants, 230–247
  care and maintenance, 242–245
  diseases, 246, 247
  insects, 246, 247
    protection during treatment for, 245
  lighting, 232, 238, 244

Houseplants (*continued*)
    propagation, 240–241
Humidity indoors, 94–95
Hyacinth, 150
Hybrid tea roses, 196, 203
Hydrangea, climbing, 41

I

Impatiens, 91
Indian turnip, 134
Indoor gardening. *See*
    Houseplants
Indoor-started plants
    annuals, 92–95
      under lights, 94
    bulbs, 154–155
      summer-blooming, 162
Informal vs. formal bulb
    gardens, 146
Injury repair for trees, 85
Inorganic fertilizers, 12
Insects. *See* Pests
Irises, 122, 124
Irrigation, drip, 10, 166
Ivy, 32, 235

J

Jack-in-the-pulpit, 134
Japanese beetles, 206
Japanese spurge, 33
Jars, strawberry, 227
    annuals in, 104–105
June-bearing strawberries,
    226
Junipers, 54, 85
    Chinese, 71

K

Kalanchoe, 236
Kerria, 54

L

Lamb's-quarters, 24
Lamium, 32, 35
Lavender, 189
Lawns, 16–27
    care and maintenance, 22
      mowing, 18
    pests, 26–27
    starting, 20–21
      seed vs. sod, 18
    types of grasses, 18
    weeds, 24–25
Leaders on trees, 80, 81,
    85
Leaf and stem cuttings
    annuals, 109
    houseplants, 240–241
Leafhoppers, 27, 185
Leaf rollers, 206
Leaves
    for fall color, 49, 70
    houseplant
      brown tips, 245, 246
Leucojum, 151
Lice, plant (aphids), 184,
    206, 246
Lighting for houseplants,
    232, 238, 244
Lights, growing plants
    under
    annuals, 94
    houseplants, 238–239
Lilacs, 49, 54
    wild (ceanothus), 51
Lilies
    daylilies, 212, 126
    hardy, 156–157
    plantain, 122
    summer-blooming, 158,
      160
      rhizomes, 163
Lilyturf, 32
Liriope, 32

Liverleaf, 133
Lunaria, 139

M

Maggots, 185
Magnolia, 74
    star, 82
Maidenhair tree (ginkgo),
    73
Map, climatic zones, 248
Maple, 74
Marigolds, 108, 132
Marjoram, 189
Marsh marigold, 132
Matted-row planting,
    method, 228, 229
Mayapple, 134
Meadow flowers, 130
Mealybug, 246
Midge, 207
Mildew, 207
Milfoil, 25
Mimosa, 74
Miniature fruit trees, 210,
    211, 214
Miniature roses, 194, 198
Mites, 27
    spider, 207, 247
Mole crickets, 27
Money plant, 139
Monkey jug plant (wild
    ginger), 133
Morning-glory, 40
Mosaic (disease), 185
Moss ball, 102
Mowing techniques, 18
Mulches, 10–11
    annuals, 108
    bulbs, 152
    perennials, 129
    roses, 201, 204
    shrubs, 59, 64
    vegetables, 182

N

Narcissus, 149
    paperwhite, forcing, 155
Nematodes, 27
NPK in fertilizer, 12

O

Oak, 68–69, 75
Old garden roses, 196
Oleander, 55
Orchids, 236
Oregano, 188
Organic fertilizers, 12
Oriental poppies, 123, 127
Ornithogalum, 151

P

Pachysandra, 30, 33
Pansies, 109, 139
Paperwhite narcissus, 155
Parsley, 188
Passionflower, 43
Peaches, 212, 219
Peach tree, miniature, 211
Pears, 212
Peas and beans, 182
Peonies, 122, 125
Peperomia, 236
Perennials, 110–135
    biennials behaving like,
      136–139
    borders, 116–117
    care and maintenance,
      128–129
    chart, bloom, 118–119
    daylilies, 121, 126
      wildflowers, 132–135
    herbs, 188, 189
    irises, 122, 124
    peonies, 122, 125

Perennials (*continued*)
poppies, 123, 127
and roses, 194
vines, 40–41, 42
wildflowers, 115, 130–131
Periwinkle, 33
Pests
fruit tree, control of, 218
houseplant, 245, 246, 247
lawn, 26–27
rose, 206–207
shrub, 64
tree, 84
vegetable and herb, 182, 184–185
Petunias, 108, 109, 152
pH, soil, 8
for lawns, 20
for shrubs, 58
Phlox, 123
woodland (wild blue phlox), 134
Pilea, 237
Pine, 75, 85
Plantain, broad-leaved, 25
Plantain lily, 122
Planters
annuals in, 91, 100–107
fruit trees in, 210, 214
strawberry jars, 104, 227
Plant lice (aphids), 184, 206, 246
Plants
ground covers, 29–35
herbs, 186–191
See also Annuals; Bulbs,
Fruits and berries;
Houseplants; Lawns;
Perennials; Roses,
Shrubs; Trees;
Vegetables; Vines
Plumbago, 40

Plums, 212, 218
Pollination of fruit trees, 212
Pollution, trees tolerant to, 71
Poppies, Oriental, 123, 127
Porcelain vine, 40
Portulaca, 109
Privacy screening, 63, 71
Propagation
annuals, 109
houseplants, 240–241
shrubs, rooting, 65
See also Dividing
Pruning
fruits
cane fruits, 222, 223
grapes, 224
roses, 202–203
shrubs, 59, 60–61, 64, 65
tools for, 14–15, 65
trees, 85
espalier, 216–217
fruit trees, 215–217
older, 82–83
young 80–81
Prunus, 55, 76
Pussy willow, 57

Q

Quack grass, 25

R

Raised beds, 166, 168, 171, 176–177
Raspberries, 220, 222, 223
Redbud, 71, 76
Repotting houseplants, 243
Rhizomes, canna, 163
Rhododendrons, 55

Rodents, protecting bulbs from, 147, 153
Root division. *See* Dividing
Root feeding of trees, 84
Rooting
annual cuttings, 109
houseplants, 240, 241
shrubs, 65
Rosemary, 189
Roses, 192–207
care and maintenance, 204–205
classification of, 196–197
diseases and insects affecting, 206–207
planting, 200–201
pruning, 202–203
Rust (disease), 207
Rye grass, cover crop, 172

S

Sage, 188
Scale (insect), 247
Seeds, starting plants from
annuals
indoors, 92–95
outdoors, 96–97
grass vs. sod, 18, 20
houseplants, 241
vegetables, 178
Self-fruitful fruit trees, 212
Shade plants
annuals, 91
ground covers, 30
perennials, 115–130
shrubs, 48
Shepherd's purse, 25
Short-season crops, 170
Shrub roses, 196
Shrubs, 44–65
care and maintenance, 64–65
hedges, 62–63

Shrubs (*continued*)
low, ground covers, 31
planting, 58–59
pruning, 59, 60–61, 64–65
Silk tree (mimosa), 74
Silver-lace vine, 41
Slopes, plants for
bulbs, 144
ground covers, 34
Slugs and snails, 185
Snowballs (viburnum), 56
Snowdrops, 150
Snowflake (leucojum), 151
Sod, 21
cutting, 22
vs. seed, 18
Sod webworms, 27
Soil and preparation, 8–9
herbs, 190
lawn, 20, 21
perennials, 117, 128
raised beds, 176
roses, 201
shrubs, 58
strawberries, 228
trees, 78
vegetables, 166, 168, 174, 182
Spider mites, 207, 247
Spirea, 56, 62
Spring-beauty, 135
Spruce, 76
Staking
annuals, 108
trees, 78–79
Star magnolia, 82
Star-of-Bethlehem, 151
Stem and leaf cuttings
annuals, 109
houseplants, 240–241
Stephanotis, 41
Strawberries, 226–229

Strawberry jars, 227
  annuals in, 104–105
Suckers, removing
  from fruit trees, 215
  from shrubs, 61
Sumac, 77
Summer bulbs, 158–163
Summer-blooming trees, 70
Sunscald, 79, 85, 218
Sweet basil, 188
Sweet william, 136, 139
Sweet william (Wild blue
  phlox), 134
Sweet woodruff, 30

T

Tansy, 189
Tea roses, hybrid, 196
  pruning 203
Thatch removal, 22
Thinning
  branches, 60
  fruits, 218–219
  seedlings, 97, 178
Thistle, Canada, 25
Thrips, 207
Thyme, 189
Tickseed, 121
Tilling, 96
Tomato plants, 182
Tools, 10, 14–15, 65
Tradescantia, 237
Transplants
  annuals, 92, 98–99
  houseplants, 243
  perennials, 124–127
  strawberries, 228, 229
Tree peonies, 125
Tree roses, 194, 198
  winter protection, 205
Trees, 66–85
  care and maintenance,
    84–85, 218–219,

Trees (continued)
  fruit
    care and maintenance,
      218–219
    planting, 214
    pruning, 215–217
    selecting, 212
  planting, 78–79, 214
  pruning, 80–83, 85, 215
    espalier, 216
    fruit trees, 215–217
    older trees, 82–83
    young trees, 80–81
Trellises for vine crops, 173
Trillium, 135
Trumpet vine, 42
Tuberous begonias, 160,
  163
Tubers, 163
Tulips, 151, 152
Tulip tree, 77

V

Vegetables, 164–185
  care and maintenance,
    182–183
  diseases and insects
    affecting, 184–185
  planning, 166, 170–171
  planting, 170, 178–179
  raised beds for, 166, 176
    168, 171, 176–177
  small-space gardens,
    174–175
  soil preparation for, 166,
    168, 174, 182
  techniques for growing
    cover cropping, 172
    double cropping, 172
    multiple harvest, 174
    vertical gardening,
      173, 176
    wide-row, 173

Viburnums, 49, 56
  highbush cranberry, 52
Vinca, 33
Vines, 36–43
  care and maintenance,
    42–43
  grapevines, 210, 211,
    224, 225
Viola, 136
Violets
  African, 237, 245
  dog-tooth, 135

W

Wake-robin (trillium), 135
Wandering Jew, 237
Warm-season crops, 170
Warm-season grasses, 18
Water and watering, 10–11
  annuals, 108
  bulbs, 152
  drip irrigation, 10, 166
  fruit trees, 218
  houseplants, 242
  lawns, 20, 22
  roses, 204
  vegetables, 182
Water sprouts, 215
Webworms, sod, 27
Weeds, 24–25, 190
Weeping cherry, 80
Weeping fig, 235
Weeping willow, 77
Weigela, 47, 56
White fly, 247
Wide-row gardening, 173
Wildflowers, 115,
  130–131
Wild Ginger, 133
Wildlife
  attracting, 70
  protecting bulbs, 147,
    153

Wildlife (continued)
  protecting fruit, 219, 223
Wild lilac, 51
Willow, 57, 77
Windflower, Grecian, 148
Window boxes, 106–107
Winged euonymus, 52
Winter aconite, 149
Winter creeper, 33
Winter protection
  perennials, 127, 129
  roses, 205
  shrubs, 65
  trees, 84, 219
Wisteria, 38, 41
Witch hazel, 57
Woodruff, sweet, 30,
Wrapping
  roses, 205
  trees, 85
    fruit trees, 218

Y

Yarrow, 25, 123
Yew, 57

Z

Zones, climatic, 248–249